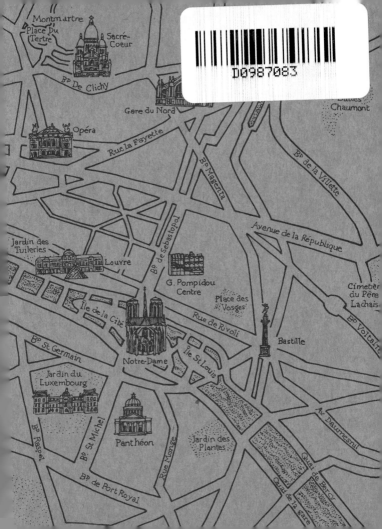

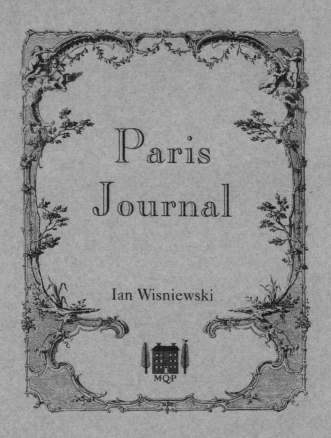

Paris
Journal

Ian Wisniewski

M·Q·P

CONTENTS

Designed by Gordon Parker & John Casey

Published by Museum Quilts (UK) Inc.
254-258 Goswell Road, London EC1V 7EB

Copyright © Museum Quilts Publications, Inc. 1997

ISBN: 1-897954-43-3

Printed and bound in Spain

The air of Paris is quite different from any other.
There's something about it which thrills and excites
and intoxicates you, and in some strange way makes
you want to dance and do all sorts of silly things. As
soon as I get out of the train, it's just as if I had
drunk a bottle of champagne.

Guy de Maupassant (1850–93), *A Night Out*

Historic Paris

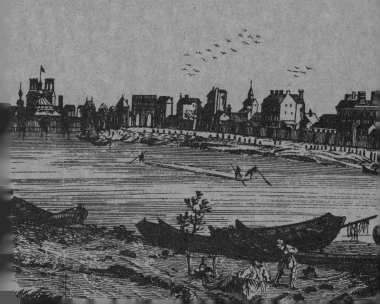

EARLY PARIS

*F*rom fishing village to sophisticated capital: over the centuries Paris has endured revolutions, sieges and wars; it has been redesigned, rebuilt and regenerated, but always thrives on its indomitable spirit.

The **Ile de la Cité** is the heart of Paris. It was first inhabited 2000 years ago by Celtic tribes, of which the most prominent were the Parisii (boat people). Conquered by Julius Caesar in 55BC when still a fishing village, it was renamed Lutetia. Julius Caesar described the Ile de la Cité as 'Lutetia Parisiorum', meaning 'the mud huts of the Parisii'. Abbreviations over the centuries yielded the current name.

The Romans extended Lutetia from the Ile de la Cité to the Left Bank, providing a forum, baths and amphitheatre (on the site of the Odéon). The legacy, including parts of the Roman baths, can be seen in the **Musée de Cluny**, and in the open air at **Arènes de Lutèce**. Built in the 2nd century, this stadium was used for theatrical performances and gladiatorial combat. It was rediscovered in 1869 during

Baron Haussmann's road-building programme.

Over the years Lutetia turned to Christianity under the Roman Gauls, as the new religion spread. During the time that the Franks held the city the populace became more educated than ever before, due to ecclesiastical influence. This led to increased church building and the development of abbeys into huge land-holding organisations. The Abbey of **St-Germain-des-Prés** owned a vast acreage of land in the city, as did many others. With the growth of religious stability the city flourished, until around 845, when Paris was ransacked by invading Vikings and rule passed to more brutish kings. Near the end of the 10th century Hugh Capet (r.987–96) managed to secure control over all of what was now France and made Paris his capital.

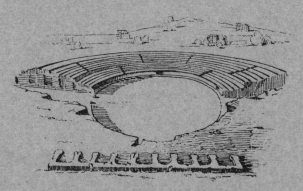

Amphitheatre in the Rue Monge

PLANNING NOTES

MEDIEVAL PARIS
900–1461

*D*uring the medieval period Paris evolved into the true heart of France: a city where politics, trade and intellectual and theological study were vigorously pursued. It was in this period that the University of Paris grew to be a major centre of European learning.

Hugh Capet was the first elected monarch of France, coming to the throne in 987. In the following years Paris expanded rapidly, even though Parisians were paralysed with fear that the end of the world would come with the end of the first millennium.

Religion received a boost from massive donations made to the churches in gratitude for the world having been spared from destruction. The spirit of religious fervour continued in subsequent centuries and Gothic spires began to rise on the Paris skyline. The **Basilica of St-Denis**, **Notre Dame** and **Sainte-Chapelle** embodied the aesthetic style of medieval Paris. As the **Sorbonne** and other colleges were established as part of the new University of Paris, the Left Bank consolidated its position as the intellectual centre of the city.

Royal power and prestige grew as Philip Augustus (r.1179–1223) made his mark on the city by building a new stone wall around the **Faubourgs** (parts of which can be seen in the **Marais** and the **Latin Quarter**), and establishing a new royal fortress at the **Louvre**. The first harbour was built in 1148 (on the Right Bank). He also created **Les Halles**, the first permanent covered market, and paved a number of the city's muddy streets.

Under Louis IX (r.1226–70) and Philip the Fair (r.1285–1314) Paris continued to grow and expand. Trade flourished and city traders and merchants created powerful and influential guilds.

Charles V (r.1364–80) constructed the **Bastille**, then a fortress, and extended the city walls. As the Hundred Years' War with England – which began in 1337 and coincided with a terrible plague known as the Black Death – drew to a close, the English took Paris in 1420 and King Henry VI of England was crowned King of France in Notre Dame in 1430. But the course of history was reversed when in 1436 Charles VII of France (r.1422–61) finally won Paris for the French. The new-found stability saw a return to prosperity, at least for the more privileged citizens.

Medieval Paris

The Latin Quarter

The Latin Quarter on the Left Bank emerged in Roman times as a place to live and trade, taking the overflow population from areas already established nearby. It was not until the Middle Ages that the area's association with education began to develop and its reputation spread throughout Europe. Peter Abélard, one of the greatest thinkers of the 11th century, came to Paris from Brittany to study under the renowned Guillaume de Champeaux, exponent of the art of dialectic – reasoning through debate. Like others he brought many of his own students with him.

Over the centuries students congregated here and the area emerged as a centre for learning with a reputation for scholarly excellence. The University of Paris evolved from 1208 statutes governing teaching and was formally established in 1253 by Robert de Sorbon, St Louis' chaplain, with an intake of 16 theology students.

The Latin Quarter was named after the **Sorbonne** students who lived and studied here. Latin was the only language allowed in the precincts surrounding the university.

The Church provided the first tutors, and through these the Latin Quarter acquired its associations with religion. In the late 5th century the Abbey of Ste-Geneviève was established on the hilltop and in 1113 the Abbey of St-Victor was founded by Louis VI. Communities began to settle around the abbeys and a strong religious tradition emerged.

The scholastic air of the Left Bank still exists today in the crooked little medieval streets. The area has always been associated with a bohemian, artistic and intellectual lifestyle, and this is as much in evidence in the Parisians who frequent the area today as it was in the past.

Specialist booksellers, including the well-known English bookshop **Shakespeare & Co**, can be found here. This area is much visited by tourists, who are catered for by small and inexpensive restaurants and bistros, some of which feature Middle Eastern, North African and Asian cuisine.

Notes

Sainte-Chapelle

After St Louis (Louis IX, r.1226–70) bought what was believed to be Christ's crown of thorns, a section of Christ's cross and other religious relics from the Emperor of Constantinople, a suitable resting place had to be built. The result, completed in 1248, was the Gothic magnificence of Sainte-Chapelle. But for all its grandeur, the king is reputed to have paid for the relics three times the cost of building the entire church.

The 15 magnificent stained glass windows include over 1000 scenes from the Old and New Testaments – *The Last Supper* is one of the most awe-inspiring. The rose window depicts the story of the Apocalypse in over 80 different panels and is most stunning when viewed at sunset. The church spire stands 75 m (245 ft) high and is the fourth to have been built – the previous three caught fire.

St-Séverin

The University's church is St-Séverin, founded in memory of Séverin, a hermit who persuaded Cleodad, the grandson of King Clovis of the Franks, to take Holy Orders. Initially a Romanesque oratory, it was redeveloped in flamboyant Gothic style in the 13th century. The church contains a statue of its namesake, together with 14th-century stained glass windows of the apostles and a rose window.

  Le Brun redesigned the chancel in the 17th century under the patronage of 'Grande Mademoiselle' Montpensier, a cousin of Louis XIV, who left her original parish church of **St-Sulpice** after a disagreement with the priest. In all, the church took over three centuries to build and is one of the most beautiful in Paris.

Notre Dame

Pope Alexander III laid the foundation stone of the Gothic cathedral of Notre Dame in 1163 on the site of a Roman temple, but the building was not completed until 1334. Funds were provided in part by grain merchants, with stained glass windows sponsored by wealthy traders, bakers, butchers, fishmongers and watercarriers.

The three rose windows are almost 10 m (33 ft) in diameter, with the north window depicting Old Testament figures around the Virgin Mary, while the south window is based on New Testament scenes, grouped around Christ. The flying buttresses, housing statues in niches, are a perfect example of how practical measures can be turned into decorative architectural features. Many of the chapels were endowed by medieval city guilds.

Notre Dame was criticised during the Revolution as a symbol of monarchy and after Napoleon's coronation – during which he took the crown from Pope Pius VII to crown himself and Josephine – it deteriorated. Viollet-le-Duc supervised restoration work in the 1840s–60s, returning Notre Dame to its full Gothic splendour, adding the famous gargoyles in various 'grotesque' animal and devil forms.

The **Musée de Notre Dame** charts the cathedral's history, with excavated remains in the **Crypte Archéologique**. Behind Notre Dame is the **Square du Jean XXIII**.

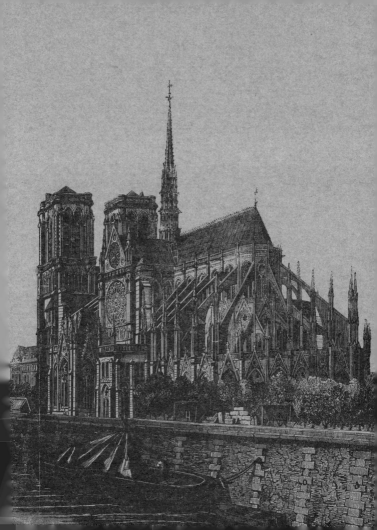

Musée de Cluny

The Musée de Cluny is housed in a fascinating building which was originally a 15th-century abbot's town house established by the Benedictine Abbey of Cluny (founded in Burgundy). Among the building's remarkable features are the **Cour d'Honneur**, a late Gothic/early Renaissance courtyard.

The house was acquired in 1833 by a prolific art collector, Alexandre du Sommerard, who used the house as a private museum. After his death it was taken over by the state in 1844 and the existing collection extended. Among this treasure-trove of medieval arts and crafts are amazing tapestries, the most famous being the series of six entitled 'The Lady with the Unicorn', as well as continental faïence and ceramics, decorative carving and woodwork, costumes, textiles and embroideries, and religious artworks such as illuminated manuscripts and stained glass.

NOTES

Louis XI

RENAISSANCE PARIS
1461–1661

*P*aris grew quickly during the Renaissance. As in other European cities the bureaucracy expanded as trade and commerce grew. Louis XII (r.1461–83) established the role of the monarchy in Paris life. He was supported in this by the guilds and by the wealthy Paris haute bourgeoisie who lived in the exclusive **Marais** district.

Francis I (r.1515–47) was the true Renaissance prince who ruled Paris and France with an iron hand. In 1526 he moved the court from the Marais into the Louvre and inaugurated a new era in the development of Paris. A great patron of the arts, he was responsible for laying the foundations for the great **Louvre** art collection, buying paintings from the masters of the Italian Renaissance. Francis was renowned for his love of ostentatious displays of wealth and his generous pensions to men of letters, who in gratitude compared him to the great Roman emperors. To pay for his excesses Francis I continually borrowed money and imposed high taxes.

Hostility flared up under Charles IX (r.1560–74), when the

Protestant Huguenots gained a foothold in the staunchly Catholic city. The Catholics responded with burning, torturing and the infamous St Bartholomew's Day massacre. On 24 August, 1572, the most influential of the king's men and many of the Protestant nobility were murdered in religious fighting that claimed more than 1500 lives .

The first Bourbon ruler of France proclaimed himself king in 1589. As a Protestant, Henri IV was not accepted by the Parisians even when, after five years of religious wars, he bowed to the will of the people and agreed to convert to Catholicism. From this time on, the Protestants blamed Henri for deserting them and the Catholics mistrusted him because they assumed that the real motive for his conversion was to win public support.

The new king began a programme of building and renovation. The aristocracy moved back to Paris and began building elegant town houses and squares, the most famous of which is the **Place des Vosges**. New neighbourhoods such as the **Ile St-Louis** rose quickly, a new bridge to the Right Bank was built (**Pont Marie**), and the Left Bank expanded – most importantly the **Quartier du Palais Royal,** where powerful ministers and wealthy bourgeois lived.

Nine-tenths of the population continued to live in acute poverty and violence was the order of the day – in 1610 Henri IV died at the hand of an assassin.

Renaissance Paris

NOTES

Place des Vosges

The oldest square in Paris, at the heart of the **Marais**, was completed in 1612. It was once the site of chivalric displays of jousting, tournaments and duels. Originally known as Place Royale, the square was built for the aristocracy and remains intact and unaltered. Nine houses line each side of the square, each side perfectly symmetrical and a testament to the architectural laws passed by the monarch.

It is one of the most beautiful squares in Paris, with its striking architectural uniformity. Place Royale was renamed Place des Vosges by Napoleon after the Revolution, as that département was the first in the Republic to pay its taxes. Number 1 was the birthplace of the writer the Marquise de Sévigné. Today No 6 houses the **Victor Hugo Museum**. Number 14 was once a town hall and is now the home of the Chief Rabbi of France.

Marie de Médici

NOTES

Palais du Luxembourg

Built between 1612 and 1622 for Marie de Médici, widow of Henri IV, the palace is in the classical style of French chateaux. While Marie lived there as a regent for her son Louis XIII (r.1610–43), she authorised elaborate decorations for her apartments. These included a cycle of 24 canvases painted by Rubens depicting the life of the queen. They were removed from the West Gallery in 1792 and placed in the **Louvre**.

The state took control of the palace in the same year and declared it to be henceforward the seat of the Directoire. A conference room and museum were added in 1814, and in the Restoration period the palace became the parliament of the Chamber of Peers. In 1834 a conference chamber, throne gallery and library were added. Today the Senate, successor to the Chamber of Peers, has its home here.

Louis XIV

ANCIEN RÉGIME
1661–1789

Louis XIV (r.1643–1715) took advantage of the country's prosperity to wage wars and spend lavishly on new plans for Paris and his new court at **Versailles**. His marriage in 1660 to Marie-Thérèse, daughter of the King of Spain, ended the rift between the two countries and freed him to take on the Dutch, Austrians and English in war.

Louis ruled with a royal authority that he believed was his divine right, assuming the soubriquet the 'Sun King'. Under his patronage and with the help of Colbert, his superintendant of finance, Paris was transformed into a city of monuments in the classical style. The medieval wall was replaced by the tree-lined **Champs Elysées** and the old gates of the wall became triumphal arches (two of which can be seen today in the **Rue Saint Denis** and **Rue Saint Mailes**). Clearly marked streets meant that a postal system became possible. The first Paris newspaper, *La Gazette,* had already begun circulation in 1631. Many hospitals, churches and public works were built in this period, which also saw the construction of great squares and open spaces such as the **Place du Carrousel**, the **Place des Victoires** and the **Place Vendôme**. The **Pont Royal** was built connecting the **Faubourg Saint-Honoré** on the Right Bank with the **Faubourg Saint Germain** on the Left. Louis was also a great patron of the arts, sponsoring the playwright Molière and creating France's national theatre, the Comédie Française. Louis also revoked the Edict of Nantes, giving Protestants the freedom of worship. However, despite the efforts of Colbert to establish an efficient tax system, Louis' economic policies were deeply unpopular and drove the country into bankruptcy.

As Louis XV (r.1715–74) was only five when he succeeded to the throne, France was ruled for a number of years by Philippe d'Orléans. In this period Paris gained a reputation for licentiousness, as illustrated in the works of writers such as the Marquis de Sade. Later it became the capital of the Age of Enlightenment. Louis' mistress, the Marquise de Pompadour, patronised Diderot, Voltaire and Montesquieu, and liberal aristocratic hostesses opened their salons for intellectual debate. In fact, on the eve of the Revolution, bourgeois Paris was smarter and more prosperous than ever.

17th-century Paris

NOTES

The Panthéon

In 1744 Louis XV, after recovering from serious illness, gave thanks to St Geneviève, the patron saint of Paris, by building a magnificent church in her honour. The Panthéon was completed in 1790, designed in neo-Classical style by French architect and the controller of the King's buildings, Jacques Germain Soufflot. The church is arranged in the form of a Greek cross and is a synthesis of Gothic and Greek architecture, taking its inspiration from the Pantheon in Rome. The church has wrestled with its identity, becoming a civic building, then reverting to a church and finally back to a civic building. The crypt is a resting place for luminaries such as Voltaire, Rousseau, Revolutionary politician Honoré Mirabeau, war-time Resistance leader Jean Moulin and Marie Curie, among many others.

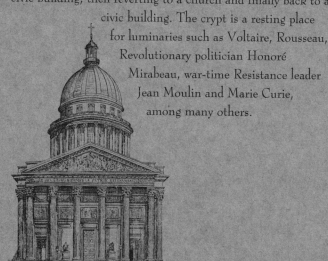

Les Invalides

A great example of Louis XIV's exuberant style is Les Invalides. Designed by Libéral Bruant and constructed between 1671–6, it was established as a hospice and home for war veterans (and now includes an Army Museum). The **Dome des Invalides**, built 1675–1706, is a chapel in the shape of a Greek cross, where Napoleon has been entombed since 1861 in a red porphyry sarcophagus. Around the tomb sculptured figures represent Napoleon's achievements.

REVOLUTION & TERROR
1789–1799

*W*hen Louis XVI (r.1774–93) came to the throne, the monarchy was deeply unpopular. Royal spending sprees, started by Francis I, continued by Henri IV and done to excess by the Sun King, had created a growing sense of injustice among the poor. Rising opposition to Louis XVI, generated by bankruptcy and food shortages and exacerbated by extravagance at court, led to the bread riots in the spring of 1789. On 20 June the commoners of the Third Estate, who had been demanding a more equitable voting system, transformed the Estates-General into a National Assembly and began discussing a constitution. The debate was taken up by the poor on the Paris streets, known as *sans culottes,* and by radical agitators in the taverns.

A crowd liberated thousands of guns from the **Invalides** on 12 July and stormed the **Bastille** prison on 14 July. Built in the 14th century, the Bastille served initially as a royal castle for Charles V, but under Cardinal Richelieu, chief minister to Louis XIII in the 17th century, it became a prison and therefore a symbol of injustice.

In October an angry crowd of Parisian women marched to Versailles to protest at the price of bread. Louis and his queen Marie Antoinette – who is supposed to have remarked 'let them eat cake' – finally agreed to be taken to Paris, where they were held in the **Tuileries** until they were executed in 1793. As the Revolution gathered momentum it became increasingly violent, leading to the Terror of 1793–4.

NOTES

Declaration of Rights

The Declaration of the Rights of Man and the Citizen in 1791 established the principles of the revolution, promising all citizens liberty, equality and fraternity.

The *Marseillaise*, anthem of the revolution, and subsequently France, was composed in May 1792 by Claude Rouget de Lisle, an officer garrisoned at Strasbourg. Its name stems from first being sung in Paris by troops from Marseilles.

Reign of Terror

> In times of peace the springs of popular
> government are in virtue, but in times of
> revolution they are both in virtue and terror.
>
> Maximilien Robespierre (1758–94), Revolutionary.

The Reign of Terror ran from April 1793 until July 1794, under the auspices of the Committee of Public Safety.

Eight months after the execution of Louis XVI (21 January, 1793) in Place de la Révolution (now **Place de la Concorde**), the Committee of Public Safety, a group of 12 men, led by Robespierre, vowed to destroy all enemies including the enemy at home.

This led to the brutal killing of over 20,000 people in Paris. The terror only ended with the execution of Robespierre himself. The revolutionary government (the Directoire) lasted five years and worked from the **Palais du Luxembourg** and the **Tuileries**.

Charlotte Corday

NOTES

Place de la Concorde

Louis XVI, Marie-Antoinette and revolutionaries such as Danton and Robespierre (having in turn been overthrown by other revolutionaries) faced the guillotine in Place de la Concorde. The square had earlier been the scene of a firework party celebrating the marriage of Louis and Marie-Antoinette. It is one of the most beautiful in Paris, with an ancient Egyptian obelisk from Luxor at its centre, balanced by two classical fountains.

She is of stately Norman figure, in her twenty-fifth year, of beautiful countenance, her name is Charlotte Corday ... About eight on Saturday morning, she purchases a large sheath-knife in the Palais Royal ... Hark, a rap again. A musical woman's voice, refusing to be rejected; it is the citoyenne who would do France a service. Marat, recognising from within, cries, Admit her ... Charlotte has drawn her knife from the sheath, plunges it with one sure stroke into the writer's heart ... His life with a groan gushes out.

Thomas Carlyle, *The French Revolution*, 1837

Napoleon Bonaparte

THE FIRST &
SECOND EMPIRES
1799–1870

*T*he Revolutionaries had fought for freedom, equality and fraternity, and in gaining these had won a society where distrust, instability and insecurity had become epidemic and the national economy stricken. With the help of the army, a new assembly ruled France and fought national wars. It was in the army that Napoleon Bonaparte (1769–1821) came to prominence. Single-minded and popular, this ambitious officer broke with the old government imposed by the Revolution, overturned it and declared himself First Consul. With the sanction of the people Napoleon asserted his form of rational government. A code of laws brought order to a better regulated, more economically stable and fairer society.

Conquering France was the first step in Napoleon's ruthless ambition to conquer Europe. Louis Napoleon's later motto 'L'Empire c'est la paix' says it all. At the heart of Napoleon's imaginary empire France ruled, and the subsequent successful invasions of neighbouring countries consolidated his power.

Only Britain held out. Aided by a series of revolts through Europe and a traitor in his own camp, Napoleon was defeated at Leipzig in 1813 and finally at the Battle of Waterloo in 1815. The monarchy was restored temporarily until 1848 when King Louis-Philippe (r. 1830–48), a reactionary, was forced to abdicate amid intolerable economic conditions and another new revolutionary spirit.

On 2 December 1851, Bonaparte's nephew, Louis Napoleon, proclaimed the Second Empire and himself Napoleon III (r. 1851–71). He thought that Paris needed to be a modern Rome, a city of grandeur and stone and so appointed Baron Haussmann to be prefect of the Seine. Haussmann had the money to work with. Trade was expanding and the Industrial Revolution created the tools for urban renewal. Under his plans, streets were widened and new boulevards created. In the process much of old Paris was lost. New buildings such as the reading room of the **Bibliothèque Nationale**, the **Jeu de Paume**, the **Orangerie**, and the remarkable **Paris Opera** (completed after his death) were added to the city. In addition there was renovation to **Notre Dame**. **Gare de l'Est** and **Gare du Nord** were opened and over 1600 hectares (4000 acres) of public parks created. One of the greatest, but largely unseen, improvements was the vast water and sewerage system that Haussmann installed.

Paris during the 2nd Empire

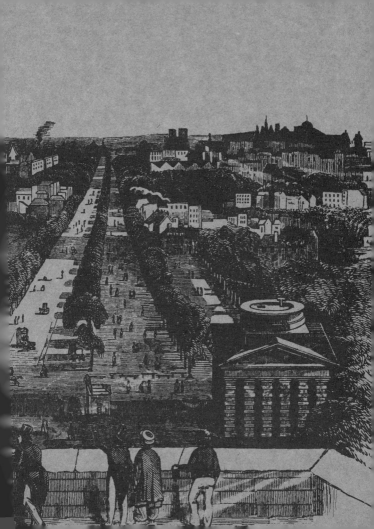

NOTES

Arc de Triomphe

'The soldier who understands Napoleon's strategy has nothing more to learn.' Fortunately, we have far more to gain, as Napoleon Bonaparte celebrated his victories in architecture. Napoleonic style is epitomised by the Arc de Triomphe, which the Emperor commissioned Chalgrin to design in 1806.

Almost 50 m (165 ft) high and 45 m (148 ft) wide, the arch was completed by Louis-Philippe in 1836, in time for Napoleon's funeral cortege to pass under it in 1840 *en route* to the **Dome of the Invalides**. Various high reliefs depict military scenes from campaigns, such as the Departure of the Army 1792 (often referred to as The Marseillaise) and the Battle of Austerlitz. Around the pediment are more than 170 shields, each bearing the name of a French military victory.

Originally five avenues converged upon the Arc de Triomphe, which Haussmann increased to an even more impressive twelve. **The Tomb of the Unknown Soldier**, interred under the arch in 1920, represents the dead of two World Wars. Victory parades for both these wars started at the Arc de Triomphe.

La Madeleine

Louis XV intended this to be a Baroque church. Napoleon thought it should be a military Temple of Glory, before changing his mind and reverting to the idea of a church. With the purpose of the building decided, its style was the next question. Louis-Philippe wanted it to resemble a Greek temple, and the ornate result includes Philippe Lemaire's pediment frieze of *The Last Judgement*, while bas reliefs on the bronze doors are based on the Ten Commandments. Corinthian columns add stature to the facade. The highly marbled interior includes a fresco above the altar depicting historical figures such as Joan of Arc and St Louis.

Arc de Triomphe du Carrousel

The Arc de Triomphe du Carrousel, inspired by the Roman arch of Septimius Severus, marks the former entrance to the **Tuileries** and was built between 1806–8. Four gilded horses looted from St Mark's Square in Venice originally crowned the arch, but were returned in 1815 and replaced by a goddess with Victory in a chariot at her side (celebrating the restoration of the monarchy). Bas reliefs depict military scenes such as the Battle of Austerlitz and Napoleon's triumphant arrival in Vienna.

NOTES

Haussmann's Paris

Appointed prefect of the Seine by Napoleon III, Baron George Haussmann (1809–91) was responsible for urban planning, and endowed Paris with much of its current grandeur. He created the familiar system of avenues and boulevards, epitomised by the 12 fashionable thoroughfares (one of which is named in his honour) radiating from the **Etoile**, with the **Arc de Triomphe** at its centre, as well as the **Champs-Elysées**, and the **Boulevards St-Michel** and

St-Germain. But urban chic came at a price, with the city's medieval elements mostly lost. Installing grandeur and memorable walks were not the sole motivation behind Haussmann's planning. With such a history of civil unrest, wide streets were deemed easier to control than narrow ones, which fostered resistance and where barricades could so easily be erected.

The Franco-Prussian War

The four-month Siege of Paris became a symbol of the Franco-Prussian War (1870–1). A terrible food shortage meant creatures in the zoo were shot and, in fact, any animal in the streets was likely to end up in the pot.

A Third Republic was declared in 1871. Following the Siege of Paris, the Communards (workers) who had tried to defend the city against the Prussians did not want to place themselves under the control of the Assemblée Nationale that had surrendered to the Prussians. The subsequent Communard uprising was dealt with brutally by French government troops, and resulted in up to 30,000 deaths.

NOTES

NOTES

LA BELLE EPOQUE
1871–1914

*F*rance's revolutionary phase ended in 1851, but the search for a political system of integrity that suited the majority went on until after the Franco-Prussian war of 1870-1. From this period on, France acquired a new-found prosperity. Coal, steel, iron and steam-powered production increased dramatically and national stability improved. The era is characterised by the Art Nouveau movement in buildings such as the **Grand Palais** and **Petit Palais**. The highly stylised and bold decorative effects in vogue at the time can be found in the iron architecture of the city – The **Eiffel Tower**, the glass roof on the **Métro**, the **Pont Alexandre III** and the **Gare du Nord,** among many others. New streets were built in the 1870s, including the **Avenue de l'Opera** and the **Boulevard Henri IV**, and the Rue de Rivoli wing was added to the **Louvre**. The city glowed with new street lights, work on the Métro began in 1890, the first department store (**Au Bon Marché**) opened and kiosks sprouted on the new boulevards. Mass consumerism was all the rage. Vieux Paris became Paris Nouveau.

The arts in the Belle Epoque

Paris oozed with excitement and dynamism. Impressionists, neo-Impressionists and abstract artists, including Monet, Degas, Renoir, Van Gogh, Cézanne, Matisse, Picasso, as well as European and American painters flocked to Paris to work, to visit and to be inspired. There was a fundamental break with the Classical and Romantic past as new generations experimented dramatically with light, colour, shape and natural themes. Ideas of impression and naturalism were expressed by writers like Emile Zola, who wrote prolifically of Paris life, and by poets like Stéphane Mallarmé and composers such as Claude Debussy and George Bizet. Theatre flourished and the fame of actresses like Sarah Bernhardt was global.

In 1911 Diaghilev brought the Russian ballet to France and in 1913 he staged the first performance of Stravinsky's ballet *Le Sacre du Printemps*, danced by Nijinsky, with settings by Picasso. The work caused uproar in the theatre.

NOTES

Sacré-Cœur

During the Siege of Paris, in the Franco-Prussian war, two of the city's Roman Catholic entrepreneurs vowed to build a church in Montmartre dedicated to the Sacred Heart if Paris was saved. They kept their word, and construction of Sacré-Cœur began in 1875, though what was initially a case of private fund raising became a State undertaking. Paul Abadie drew up Byzantine and Romanesque designs, partly inspired by St Front church at Périgueux, which he had restored, and the basilica was completed in 1914.

The dome is a principal feature of the basilica, providing wonderful views of the church's interior (including mosaics of Christ and the Sacred Heart, and statues of St Joan and St Louis), as well as exterior views across Paris. The belfry houses the **Savoyarde**, cast in 1895, and at 19 tonnes one of the world's heaviest bells.

Eiffel Tower

Universal Exhibitions provided Paris with perfect opportunities to parade its artistic and scientific élan to the world. Gustave Eiffel's Tower was only meant as a temporary spectacle for the Universal Exhibition of 1889. Initially, it was roundly condemned by aesthetes, but soon became an essential part of the Parisian scene. Entrance fees during its first year more than covered the building costs. The viewing gallery, perched at a height of 275 m (900 ft), gives panoramic views of up to 70 km (45 miles), as far as **Chartres Cathedral** on a good day. The **Jules Verne** restaurant, one of the city's finest, also serves great views. The Tour Eiffel has attracted plenty of daredevils, performing stunts such as parachuting off the top.

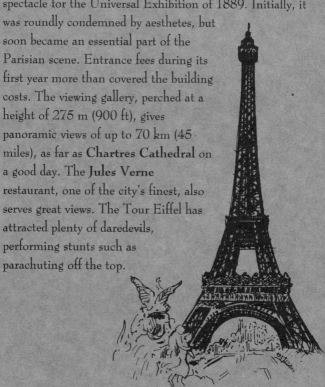

NOTES

The 20th Century

The War Years

War was declared on 3 August 1914 and, although the city was bombarded, little damage was done. The German forces came within sight of the Eiffel Tower but the French rallied and the enemy troops did not get any further. The Armistice was signed on 11 November 1918 in **Versailles**, with France regaining Alsace and Lorraine, which had been lost after the Franco-Prussian War.

The end of the First World War signified the start of the modern era. New developments and a technologically advancing society had brought motor cars in abundance to the streets and the pace of life quickened in response. This was the era of cinema, jazz clubs, the **Moulin Rouge**, the **Folies-Bergère** and the Charleston, introduced by Josephine Baker. Life became more sociable and more avant garde.

In May 1940 the German army rolled into France and within four weeks had defeated French troops. Pétain called for a ceasefire – his regime was later seen as an act of collaboration with Germany. The French Resistance began with small and individual acts of subversion and defiance, but grew into an underground movement of intelligence networks fighting continually against the Germans in collaboration with other French units and British operations. The Allies liberated Paris in August 1944, and the Armistice was signed in 1945.

The postwar era was symbolised by low-cost building, of a functional and practical purpose, with little decoration. Paris moved outwards to the suburbs.

Contemporary Paris

Construction of the business district **La Défense** began in 1955 and was alternately applauded for being high-tech, and condemned for its brutal modernism. The intensity of student riots in May 1968, against the social policies of President de Gaulle, took Paris by storm, and escalated as trade unions joined the demonstrations with strikes throughout the country. The **Pompidou Centre**, built in 1977, was another cause célèbre, with infrastructure on the exterior of the building, while the 59-storey **Tour Montparnasse** achieved new heights of derision. The bicentenary of the Revolution in 1989 was celebrated with the inauguration of a new opera house at **Place la Bastille** and a highly controversial addition to the **Louvre**, a glass and steel pyramid designed by American architect I M Pei.

NOTES

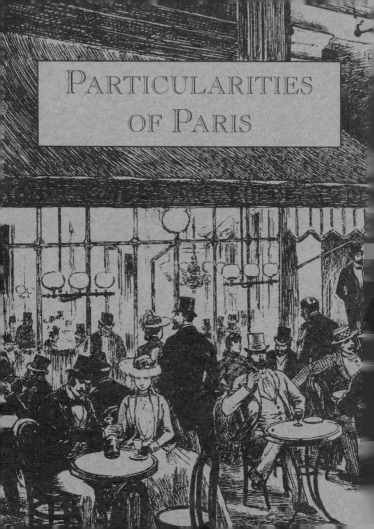

Particularities
of Paris

LOVE, ROMANCE & INFIDELITY

*P*aris is undoubtedly the city for lovers, supplying all the *mise en scène* for romance: elegant boulevards and cobbled streets, river views, ornate architectural facades, beautifully cultivated and perfectly proportioned squares, gardens and parks, some of the very finest cuisine in the most renowned restaurants and a reputation for the world's most beautiful women.

France has an endless list of romantic couples, femmes fatales and dangerous liaisons, from the ill-fated Louis XVI and Marie-Antoinette, to Napoleon and Josephine, Sartre and de Beauvoir to Catherine Deneuve and Marcello Mastroianni. Fiction and cinema have contributed to this notion, encouraging the associations and image to live on with work such as *Last Tango in Paris*, *Jules and Jim*, *The Hunchback of Notre Dame*, *Swann in Love* and Flaubert's classic *Sentimental Education*. Then there are the famous mistresses, most famous of all Madame de Pompadour, Madame du Barry and La Dame aux Camélias.

Abélard and Héloise

The Ile-de-la-Cité provided a romantic rendezvous for Pierre Abélard, a young monk who matured into a renowned 12th-century theologian, and Héloise, 17-year-old daughter of a canon named Pierre Fulbert. The canon was horrified to discover their love affair and ordered Abélard to leave Paris. He did, taking Héloise with him to Brittany, where she gave birth to their son. Fulbert's revenge was having Abélard castrated. Abélard's countermove was to use his influence to have Fulbert dispossessed of all property, before retiring to a monastery. Héloise took up long-term residence in a convent. After decades apart, Abélard and Héloise were finally reunited, but only in a tomb at **Père-Lachaise Cemetery**.

Le Tombeau d' Abeillard

NOTES

NOTES

Sentimental Conversation

In the old solitary frozen park
two forms just passed and vanished in the dark.
Their lips were soft and slack, their eyes were dead,
and one could scarcely hear the words they said.
In the old lonely park nipped by the frost,
two spectres have called back the past they lost.

   Do you remember our old ecstasies?
   Why would you have me waken those
                   memories?
   When you hear my name does your heart
             always glow?
Do you always see my soul in dreams? – No.
   Ah, the good days of joy unspeakable
when our lips mingled! – That is possible.
   How blue the sky was then, and hope beat high!
   But hope fled, vanquished, down the gloomy
             sky.
Even so they walked through the wild oats, these
             dead,
and only the night heard the words they said.

         Paul Verlaine (1844–96)

Love pavilions

Holding hands on a park bench can be the most romantic experience. But particular settings, acting as a visual aphrodisiac, can make the heart beat even faster. Paris excels in this department. After all, how many cities cater for *l'amour* to the extent of providing Love Pavilions? Built in the **Bois de Boulogne** in the late 18th century, together with various romantic accessories such as a pagoda, waterfalls and grottoes, the **Chateau Bagatelle** is the sole survivor, and is now used principally for horticultural exhibitions. What a pity! At least the gardens and ponds continue a spirit of romance.

Edward VIII and Wallis Simpson

What price love? He became King Edward VIII in January 1936, but the British government's objections to the woman he loved, American divorcee Wallis Simpson, led to his abdication at the end of the year. They married in June 1937 in France, as the Duke and Duchess of Windsor, spending some of their exile in a mansion in the Bois de Boulogne. The Windsors' last permanent residence, from 1951–1986, when the Duchess died (the Duke died in 1971), was a 19th-century 'Petit Trianon' style house set in 1.6 hectares (4 acres) on **Route du Champ d'Entraînement**. The house is now a private residence, and is maintained exactly as it was in the heyday of the Windsor's and is never open to the public.

GASTRONOMY

*P*aris is the world's gastronomic capital, with an unrivalled range of restaurants, brasseries, bistros and cafés. Parisian chefs pride themselves on providing the best, and that is what their customers demand regardless of the price. Serial execution of aristocrats during the Revolution left many chefs without an employer. The solution was to open their own restaurants in Paris, catering for citizens who had prospered through the Revolution (thus replacing the aristocracy). Liberty, equality and fraternity also included the right to eat well.

Famous chefs such as Antonin Carême (who pre-Revolution cooked for kings and emperors), ran modest eating places which served the proletariat. A new public with a taste for good food was found and *haute cuisine* grew alongside *cuisine bourgeoise*. Throughout the decades Parisians have had the good sense and fortune to demand the freshest ingredients and best wines, which continue to arrive daily from all over France. Motto: Book ahead!

Wine

Champagne is the only wine that leaves a woman
beautiful after drinking it.
Madame de Pompadour (1721–64)

In victory you deserve it, in defeat you need it.
Napoleon (1769–1821)

French wine is reputed throughout the world, not surprising
considering that grapes have been cultivated and harvested in
southern France from time immemorial. Wine is more than a
joy to Parisians, it is a way of life. Paris also declares its own
vintage with a vineyard in Butte, the hill of Montmartre,
called **Clos Montmartre**. The harvest only
amounts to several hundred bottles, but
that does not limit the harvest
celebrations in October. For a
more academic appraisal of wine,
the **Musée du Vin** charts the
history of wine-making within
atmospheric cellars.

The café at the Palais Royal in 1880

Breakfast

Missing breakfast is frequently seen as an easy way of saving time and calories, but if it means sacrificing a 'café complet' then it really is a false economy. This typical Parisian breakfast usually comprises orange juice, coffee, croissants or brioches, confiture and toasted bread.

While the croissant is such an emblem of French indulgence, its source was actually Budapest. In 1686 the Turks, who were besieging Budapest, planned to enter the city by digging tunnels. Bakers on the early shift heard sinister noises and, raising the alarm, foiled the Turkish plot. The bakers were upheld as the city's saviours, and their reward was the honour of devising a commemorative pastry, the only condition being that it was crescent-shaped, reflecting the emblem on the Ottoman flag. It was a sweet taste of victory.

Dinner

While best known for romantic and swashbuckling stories, such as *The Three Musketeers*, Dumas was also a gastronome. Keeping a private dining room at Maison Doré in Paris was one of his foibles, though his *Grand Dictionnaire de Cuisine* is more entertaining than factual.

> Dinner is a principal act of the day that can only be carried out in a worthy manner by people of wit and humour; for it is not sufficient just to eat at dinner. One has to talk with a calm and discreet gaiety. The conversation must sparkle like rubies in the entremets wines, it must be delightfully suave with the sweetmeats of the dessert, and become very profound with the coffee.
>
> Alexandre Dumas (1802–70)

NOTES

Street food

> The appetite grows as you eat.
> Francois Rabelais (1494–1553)

Croque monsieur is the ultimate Parisian sandwich. The ingredients are simple: toasted bread, ham and gruyère cheese (or béchamel sauce). *Croque madame* means an egg on top.

Crêpes are another example of 'superior fast food', which can just as easily be savoury as sweet, with classic fillings such as béchamel sauce flavoured with mushrooms, seafood, or ham, while adding scoops of ice cream, jam, or just a squeeze of lemon juice and sugar makes an instant dessert. The tangerine-flavoured *crêpe suzette* is thought to be a *fin-de-siècle* Parisian invention. A similar range of fillings can be applied to the quick and easy waffle, which also relies on a batter of eggs, flour and milk.

NOTES

Restaurants for all

The second half of the 19th century saw the growth of enormous wealth, which of course meant more restaurants. The legion of workers who helped create the wealth, but did not actually share in it, ate daily in 'bouillons' (cheap bistros), particularly as their accommodation usually lacked cooking facilities.

In the 1930s regulars to these bouillons, such as Edith Piaf and Maurice Chevalier, stored their own napkins and cutlery in small boxes at the restaurant, which brought the bill down even further. Of course, having little money did not mean customers tolerated any compromise.

Brasseries

With phylloxera epidemics ravaging French vineyards, beer and brasseries (the French word for 'brewery') came to the fore in the 1880s. Their aim was to have a quick turnover of well-fed customers, but the interior decoration also mattered. **Bofinger** is a fine example, with a stained-glass dome in its central dining room accompanied by decorative tiles and objets. Many Parisian brasseries were started by people from Alsace. They arrived after Germany annexed Alsace-Lorraine in 1870, bringing with them hearty fare such as choucroute (sauerkraut with sausages and various cuts of meat).

Bistros

Cossacks wanting speedy attention in bars and small restaurants, during the Russian occupation of Paris in 1815, used to shout 'bistro', meaning 'quick' in Russian. Now a thoroughly French term, it refers to informal, local eateries.

The 'zinc' (bar counter) is a focal point of many cafés. Making its debut in modest 19th-century bars, the aim was to serve people as quickly as possible. Standing at the counter naturally encourages a faster turnaround than sitting at a table, where prices are usually at a premium.

Pastis

A carafe of water surrounded by glasses of anise is a classic sight on café tables. Aniseed drinks have been around since the Middle Ages. Pernod emerged in the late 18th century. A recipe for wild herbs infused in alcohol, acquired by Major Henri Dubied and his son-in-law Henri-Louis Pernod, was originally sold as an absinthe. The Pernod brand name was incorporated to distinguish it from similar drinks, which then became known as 'pastiches', and abbreviated into the current reference, pastis. Aniseed drinks were *de rigueur* in 1890s' café society. However, absinthe also induced trance-like states, a fact that emerged in some highly publicised murder cases. All was revealed when wormwood, an ingredient in absinthe, was found to be toxic and banned in 1915. The drinks simply continued to be sold without it.

NOTES

CAFÉ LIFE

*T*he joy of Paris is never being far from a café, and waiters will not mind if you spend hours over a single coffee. A café is a social event, whether it is a tête-à-tête with friends or being *tout seul*; reading, writing, thinking, dreaming and, of course, seeing who else is there. 'Look-who's-passing-by' is another absorbing occupation, with pavement tables a perfect observatory. At any time of the day you can quench your thirst with one of the classics, a *café au lait* (coffee with milk), expresso, double expresso or a *decafeiné*, tea, *tisane* (herbal tea), *une pression* (beer), *une kir* (white wine with *cassis* – blackcurrant liqueur), a *citron pressé* (lemonade – adding your own water and sugar), *un chocolat chaud* (hot chocolate) or Orangina (France's most popular soft drink).

Breakfast is the busiest and most popular time of day for cafés – hardly surprising considering the ritual of croissants or *pain au chocolat* , hot chocolate or coffee and fresh orange juice that most Parisians take for granted.

Café society

Paris was the birthplace of café society, and indeed the world's first café, **Le Procope**, was opened in Paris in 1686 by Francesco Procopio, a Sicilian. Its ornate decor attracted an exclusive, bohemian clientele (and cafés were then an exclusively male domain). Le Procope's regulars included Rousseau, Benjamin Franklin and Voltaire, who apparently drank up to 40 cups of coffee flavoured with chocolate on a daily basis. Le Procope still thrives, and has matured over the centuries into a restaurant.

NOTES

HAUTE COUTURE

*C*lothes and accessories have always made social distinctions, and society has been governed by fashion dictates for centuries. The demise of the Second Empire signalled the grand entrance of *haute couture* and the end of the seamstress and private dressmaker of the 19th century, largely through the rise of two fashion icons.

Charles Worth moved to Paris from London in 1845, working as a draper before opening his salon in 1858. Worth acquired a reputation for impeccable tailoring. By assembling collections in advance, Worth established fashion seasons. Meanwhile, Jacques Doucet's arrival at a lingerie shop in 1875 soon saw it offering couture, and patronised by Sarah Bernhardt.

Just 23 couture houses are listed with France's Fédération Français de la Couture. The rules are rigid. Most fashion houses of such international acclaim are based in the **Rue du Faubourg St-Honoré**, including Chanel, Dior, Versace, Saint Laurent and Lacroix.

Nº 3986. bis

Modes de Paris

Mars 1875.

Journal des Demoiselles

ET PETIT COURRIER DES DAMES RÉUNIS

Paris, Boulevart des Italiens 1

Modes de E. Mellier de Mr Brioud : Rue Richelieu 76

NOTES

Fashion shows

As inhabitants of one of the world's most beautiful cities, what would you expect of Parisians other than the height of style and elegance? Meanwhile, 'supply and demand' keep perpetuating each other, ensuring that every shopper and every designer finds stylistic fulfilment in Paris.

There are fashion shows in Milan, London and New York, but it is the Paris collections that are paramount. Parisian women are famed for their impeccable chic and the fashion seasons are a commercial advantage for designers as they launch an entire new look in every collection. None of the fashion set wants to be seen wearing 'quelque chose' from last season – it would be far too embarrassing.

Christian Dior

Christian Dior began work running a gallery in Paris, exhibiting artists such as Salvador Dali and Jean Cocteau. That was in the 1920s, and it took another ten years before he started selling his own fashion illustrations and designs to magazines. He joined the fashion house of Lucien Lelong in 1941, and began designing, presenting his own collection in 1947, which created a sensation.

> The air of Paris is truly the air of couture.
> Christian Dior (1905–57), couturier

Chanel

'Fashion passes, style lives on,' said Coco Chanel (1883–1971). Chanel ruled the world couture scene between the war years dictating new concepts in clothes. She is famous for her suits, cardigans, black dresses and her perfume.

Hermès

Having first specialised in horse-harnesses and saddles, the advent of the motor car and demise of horse-drawn carriages saw Hermès refocus its expertise for leather, initially producing wallets, travelling cases and handbags. The **Hermès Museum** is at the Faubourg St-Honoré shop.

Musée de la Mode et du Costume

Formerly the home of fashion-lover Duchesse Maria de Ferrari Galliera, the **Palais Galliera** now houses the Musée de la Mode et du Costume. Exhibits span 18th-century to contemporary fashion, with clothes donated by designers and fashionable figures such as Princess Grace of Monaco. The 30,000 costumes and 70,000 accessories change twice a year and usually focus on the career of a designer or themes from the past. The fashion section of the **Musée des Arts Décoratifs**, in the Rue de Rivoli, pays homage to various Parisian designers, while the **Musée des Arts de la Mode**, also within the **Louvre**, has a vast wardrobe of couture and fashion accessories.

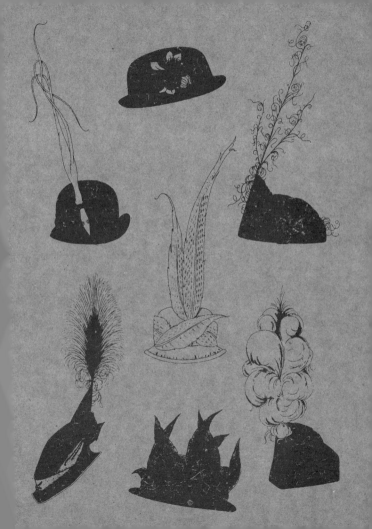

SHOPPING

*R*ue du Faubourg St-Honoré is one of the most famous addresses in Paris that all serious shoppers hurry to. The entire city is like a 'grand magasin', however, with plenty of other 'essential destinations', such as **Boulevard Haussmann**, **Rue de la Paix**, **Avenue Montaigne**, **Avenue George V**, **Rue Bonaparte** and the **Champs Elysées**.

For smaller designer shops, cute gift shops or one-offs don't miss the **Marais**. The **Rue des Rosiers** and the **Rue des Francs-Bourgeois** are especially lively and colourful, particularly on Sunday afternoons. For good ready-to-wear designer clothes, shoes and bags, head for the Left Bank. The area between **Boulevard St-Germain** and **Place St-Sulpice** is a shopper's dream: here you'll find all the chic names like Max Mara, Paraboot, Prada, Sonia Rykiel and lots more. The **Rue du Bac** is a winding street full of great little shops and a few excellent large ones such as the **Conran Shop** and the elegant and bustling **Au Bon Marché**.

Another interesting stop in this area is a branch of the **Compagnie Française de l'Orient et de la Chine**, where you can find wonderful one-of-a-kind clothing, silk shirts, gorgeous scarves, tableware and furniture.

The big department stores with their huge and varied selection include **Galeries Lafayette, Au Printemps** and **La Samaritaine. Monoprix/Uniprix** has stores throughout Paris and carries less expensive items. The **Carrousel du Louvre** is a terrific underground complex full of tasteful shops located in the **Grand Louvre**. It is worth a spin if you can cope with the crowds.

For books, **FNAC** stores and **Gibert Joseph** are the main chains. English books can be found at **Brentano's** and a **WH Smith** and a smaller selection is available from the atmospheric wood-panelled **Galignani**.

For antiques, spend a pleasant afternoon wandering around the galleries of **Quai Voltaire** in the **Carré Rive Gauche**, where the clusters of tiny antique shops include many specialists among their number. If art is what you're looking for, the northern part of the **Marais** is where the new generation of artists have set up shop, converting old warehouses into galleries. The galleries around **St-Germain-des-Prés** are less contemporary in style and tend to give equal emphasis to sculptural works in their exhibition space.

NOTES

Chaumet

Napoleon I's coronation in 1804 meant a major commission for Chaumet, the jeweller established in 1780 on Rue Saint-Honoré. Britain's Queen Victoria, too, was devoted to graceful sprays of bejewelled flowers, which were Chaumet's forte. The **Chaumet Museum** is at Place Vendôme.

Cartier

'Jeweller to Kings, King of Jewellers,' was Edward VII's description of Cartier – his company delivered 27 tiaras for the king's coronation in London in 1902. Cartier designed the first watch on a leather strap for the Brazilian aviator Alberto Santos-Dumont in 1904, while a panther set on a bracelet watch helped the Duchess of Windsor check the time from 1948 onwards.

Christofle

Charles Christofle, a silversmith since 1830, developed advanced silverplating techniques that made smart tableware far more affordable for middle-class Parisians. As centrepieces and various accessories came into vogue, so the company extended its repertoire and its customer profile, becoming official supplier to King Louis-Philippe, while Napoleon III ordered complete dinner services.

Perfume

Perfume really came to the fore in Europe in the Middle Ages after the Crusaders brought back a selection of exotic ingredients, and the know-how, from the East. Today many couturiers have extended their lines of personal accessories to include fragrances.

Guerlain

Created by Guerlain especially for the Empress Eugénie in 1853, Eau Impériale's citrus and rosemary notes were so attractive to her husband, Napoleon III, that he appointed Guerlain his official supplier. Formed in 1828, Guerlain is the oldest French perfume house.

NOTES

Vuitton

Louis Vuitton came to Paris on foot from his home in the Jura mountains, and began his career as a layetier, packing clothes for wealthy patrons in hotels. That led to his appointment as layetier to Empress Eugénie of France in 1852. He opened his own luggage shop several years later, displaying a newly designed flat-topped trunk which was to change the style and fashion of luggage and was so much more practical than the bulky chests people still used. The growth of rail travel and the corresponding need for well-designed trunks became the foundation of his empire. An ingenious valise that unfolds into a camp bed was designed for Congo explorer Savorgnan de Brazza in 1876.

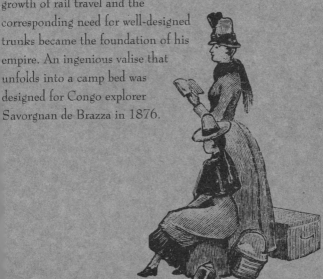

MARKETS

*P*aris is a shopper's paradise and the city's markets are a treat to be experienced. Parisians shop daily for food to be sure to obtain the freshest produce, although be aware that this is not always a guarantee of good quality.

From the hustle and bustle of the busiest food markets to the picturesque green wooden stalls selling antiquarian and second-hand books and prints on the Left Bank, the city's markets are renowned for offering a wide selection of products, selling anything from fresh flowers, stamps and art to bric-a-brac at one of the city's many flea markets.

Most markets start early, so if you're looking for something specific be prepared to get up in time to catch the best buys. This is one of the best ways to see Parisians going about daily life and an ideal way to capture the sounds, aromas and sights that are the true essence of Paris. Many markets operate on a Tuesday to Saturday basis, most particularly those selling food. **Rue de Lévis**, **St-Germain** and **Rue de Seine** are just a few markets worth trying.

Specialist markets

For those with flowers in mind, the **Marchés aux Fleurs** at Place de la Madeleine, Place des Ternes and Place Louis Lepine assault the senses with a visual feast of colour and fragrance.

See birds at the **Marché aux Oiseaux** on the Ile de la Cité each Sunday. This market replaces the flower market held here throughout the week. It is a riot of birdsong and exotica.

The **Marché aux Timbres,** held Thursday, Saturday and Sunday, is an excellent source of unusual and old stamps and postcards. It is a must for avid collectors and a pleasant place to browse.

Each weekend farmers from the surrounding countryside flock into Paris to the **Marché Biologique** to sell organic vegetables, fruit, home-baked bread, goat's cheese, cider and free range poultry.

For bookworms the Left Bank is overflowing with bookshops selling every type of book, comic, magazine and journal, both new and secondhand. The wooden stalls or *bouquinistes* along the Seine are a good starting point and, if you're lucky, real bargains are waiting to be found.

Fabrics unusual and exotic can be purchased Monday to Saturday at inexpensive prices at the **Marché St-Pierre**. This is the market the professionals use so its worth while spending the time looking for bargains for next season's creations.

The fish market at les Halles about 1900

NOTES

Flea markets

Paris has three permanent flea markets, all selling the widest collections of goods from antiques, furniture, clothes and books to bric-a-brac. The **Puce de St-Ouen** is the most famous and colourful of all markets. The **Marché Dauphine** sells antiques, the **Marché Biron** stocks unusual Second Empire pieces. **Marché Malik** is the most upbeat of all the markets, selling Americana and 1960s gear. Whilst not comparable in terms of size, the **Puce de Vanves** and the **Puce de Montreuil** stock similar objects to St-Ouen.

Les Bouqinistes

So as not to obstruct river views, the height of *les bouqinistes* (river-bank stalls) is strictly governed. Their contents, however, are not, being something of a lucky dip, with plenty of kitsch on offer. Charming postcards, antiquarian books and prints are waiting to be discovered, not to mention the type of ephemera that is an essential souvenir of Paris.

NIGHTLIFE

*P*arisian nights are not intended for sleeping. That seems such a waste when there is so much entertainment to be enjoyed, whether it is a show or a nightclub to dance the night away. Everyone knows the **Folies-Bergère** (32 Rue de Richer), which has had plenty of time to establish its reputation, being open since 1869. The **Moulin Rouge** (82 Boulevard de Clichy) is thought to be where the can-can was invented. The most famous nightclub must be **Régine's** (9 Rue de Ponthier). Nightclubs come and go, but Régine's just keeps on going. For a spectacular cabaret show the **Lido** is the place to go.

In recent years the trend has been towards music bars and cafés-concerts, more elegant and sophisticated than the traditional reputation of the nightclub. **Le Doobie's** attracts young Parisians. **La Calvados**, a small bar, attracts a set of regulars for cocktails and entertainment.

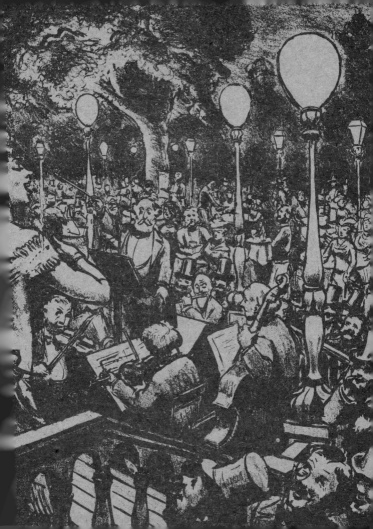

MUSEUMS, GALLERIES & ARTISTS

A museum lover's paradise

Paris has museums that span the world's finest art works – paintings, drawings, sculptures, tapestries, religious art, tribal art and so on – as well as the most important artistic movements – Gothic, Renaissance, Baroque, Rococo, Impressionism, Belle Epoque, Art Nouveau, Expressionism, and Post-Modernism. With almost 100 collections to visit, covering every aspect of history, Paris has in the last 20 years become a museum-lover's paradise.

Some museums, such as the **Louvre** and the **Musée de Cluny**, are such historic buildings that the contents are effectively a museum within a museum. Others, like the **Pompidou Centre**, are so progressive that only time will tell whether their 'merits' will still be applauded in the future.

The history of Paris and its culture are the focus of some museums. Others exhibit the lifestyles of the city's celebrated inhabitants. The former homes of writers and artists such as Victor Hugo, Honoré de Balzac, Pablo Picasso, Auguste Rodin and even Edith Piaf provide a more immediate setting in which to trace their lives and artistic achievements. From the humblest presentations to the world's largest museum, from arts and crafts, to natural history and fine art, the museums of Paris contain something for everyone.

NOTES

The Louvre

The Louvre was originally built by Philip-Augustus at the end of the 12th century as a fortress (which is appropriate for a building that now houses one of the world's finest art collections). In 1360 it became a royal residence under Charles V, and was remodelled into a Renaissance chateau in the 16th century. When Louis XIV decided to move the court to Versailles in 1682, the Louvre was given to the Academy of Art, and provided accommodation for artists. The first gallery opened to the public in 1793, after which the Louvre collection began to evolve. It is now the world's largest museum.

The museum is so vast that it is impossible to try to see everything in one day. The list of artworks, sculptures, antiquities and objects is endless. The Louvre is a shrine to European art, covering the period 1400–1900, and contains some of the world's most famous works: Leonardo da Vinci's *Mona Lisa*, Rembrandt's self-portraits, Vermeer's *Lacemaker*, Michelangelo's *Slaves*, Botticelli's *Venus and the Graces*, Géricault's *The Raft of the Medusa*, portraits by Holbein, J M W Turner's *Landscape with a River*, and Fragonard's *The Bathers*, and a great many more. Whilst the collection of artworks dates back to the Middle Ages, the museum's collection of antiquities starts in 7BC. The Egyptian, Roman, Etruscan and Greek antiquities include sculpture, brickwork, carvings, decorated objects, statues, a Sphinx and fragments of the Parthenon. The works collectively offer an impressive insight into ancient life.

The Louvre's collection of objets d'art is awe-inspiring. Among the most spectacular of these world-renowned pieces are the **Hunt of Maximilian** tapestries of 1530; the French coronation jewels of Napoleon; one of the world's purest diamonds; stone plates dating from 1AD inset with precious stones and representations of gold dolphins; Queen Marie-Antoinette's steel and bronze writing desk; clocks, miniatures, silverware, glassware, bronzes, carved ivory and cabinets inlaid with copper and tortoise-shell.

The Louvre is one of France's most revered institutions and is never far from the public's consciousness. In 1981 plans, now carried out, for a new entrance to the Louvre incorporating a great glass pyramid set in juxtaposition to the ancient surrounding buildings came under public scrutiny and much debate between traditionalists and modernists.

The Louvre

Musée Gustave Moreau

Gustave Moreau, famed for his symbolic artworks, developed a museum for his work with the intention of bequeathing his collection of 1000 oil paintings and 7000 watercolours to the State. Moreau's work are fantastical depictions of biblical and mythological figures. His art expresses a powerful and imaginative spiritual vision of life.

Musée Delacroix

Born near Paris in 1798, Eugène Delacroix was never a painter who subscribed to the artistic conventions of his time. His individuality yielded a highly Romantic genius and he is widely regarded as the link between old master artworks and the newer style taking shape at the time. The house where he lived, at 6 Place de Fürstenberg, from 1857 to his death in 1863, is now the Delacroix Museum. It features various pictures as well as the artist's studio. His Romantic image of the Revolution, *Liberty Leading the People*, is in the Louvre.

Delacroix's studio in 1853

Musée d'Orsay

A comprehensive collection of Impressionist paintings hangs in the Musée d'Orsay, a former railway station that was once a condemned building but successfully transformed into a museum in 1986. The museum houses an impressive collection of artworks from the 1848–1914 period, and was moved here from the **Louvre** to be better displayed and set in context with exhibits on social and political themes of the day, as well as advances in technology.

The Impressionist artists aimed to capture the impression and effect of light on the landscape, but their work was considered unintelligible and unfinished when their first paintings appeared in the 1860s. It was not until the 1880s that Impressionism was accepted as *bona fide* art by the establishment. Claude Monet's *Impression: Sunrise,* exhibited in 1872, helped establish the movement's name, and reputation. Urban landscapes were also a source of inspiration, with Camille Pissaro celebrating Parisian thoroughfares, while Monet did the same for the Gare St Lazare.

In offering such a relatively short span of art history the museum is able to give space to the diversity of each artistic movement without compromising the artists intentions. The focus of the museum is the artworks and sculpture on display, with secondary exhibits of architecture, posters, cinematic history, books and newspapers.

Exhibits of world renown include Manet's *Le Déjèuner sur l'Herbe*, Degas' *Girl Dancer, aged 14*, Gauguin's *Arearea*, Carpeaux' *The Dance*, and Cézanne's *The Bridge at Maincy*. Not to be missed are works by Monet, Van Gogh, Delacroix, Guillaume and the Art Nouveau works that were popular throughout Europe in the early part of the 20th century.

> Beauty in art is truth bathed in the impression. If you have been sincere in your emotion you will be able to pass it onto others ... You must detach yourself from what you know of old masters or of contemporaries. Only in this way will you do work of real feeling. Follow your convictions. It is better not to exist than to be the echo of other painters.
>
> Corot (1796–1875), painter

The Grand Palais

Greatly admired for its use of metal and glass, the Grand Palais was built for the Universal Exhibition of 1900, and now exhibits French painting and sculpture. It also includes a **Planetarium** and **Science Museum**.

Its diminutive partner, the **Petit Palais**, was also built for the Exhibition and now houses the **Musée des Beaux-Arts de la Ville de Paris**, with collections of medieval objets d'art, 18th-century furniture, paintings and drawings and 19th-century art.

NOTES

Musée Picasso

Although Spanish, Pablo Picasso (1881–1973) spent much of his life in France in protest against General Franco's regime. The palatial Musée Picasso is housed in the Hôtel Salé, originally built in 1656 for a salt tax collector, Aubert de Fontenay. The collection was 'donated' by the artist's family to the nation in lieu of death duties.

The museum houses the largest collection of Picasso's work in the world as well as Picasso's private collection of his contemporaries' work. The exhibition changes constantly, although the work is displayed roughly in chronological order, covering his Blue, Pink, Cubist and Neo-classical styles. Among the most highly regarded exhibits are his *Self-Portrait*, *Two Women Running on the Beach* and *The Kiss*. The garden also acts as a sculpture gallery.

Musée des Invalides

Although devoted to the history of the army from medieval times to modern day, many of the exhibits are of social, historical and political significance. The collection includes uniforms, artworks, photography, the Resistance and Free France exhibits, and model fortresses.

Musée Carnavalet

The Musée Carnavalet offers a good starting point for anyone wishing to study the history of Paris. It includes an extensive collection of prehistoric archaeological finds, Bronze and Iron Age remains, Roman objects and remains from the Merovingian and Carolingian eras. The various artefacts help recount the history of Paris, with different rooms devoted to subsequent eras: the Middle Ages, Renaissance Paris, the religious wars, Paris under the Ancien Régime and during the 17th and 18th centuries.

Musée National d'Histoire Naturelle

In 1793 this national museum of natural history opened its doors to the public with the intention of preserving and expanding its then current collection, acting as a centre of research and to teach and educate. Today its objectives are still the same. The development of animal and fossil life, the evolution of man and the history of ornithology can be studied here using the massive collections in the various galleries.

Notes

Musée d'Art Moderne de la Ville de Paris

Parisian vistas have always inspired painters. Henri Matisse (1869–1954) was among many who have painted the Seine; Robert Delaunay (1885–1941) was similarly captivated by the Eiffel Tower. Their works can be seen in the Musée d'Art Moderne de la Ville de Paris, which has a magnificent collection of 20th-century art, including Fauvism, Cubism and Surrealism.

Musée de Montmartre

In the late 19th and early 20th century, Montmartre offered cheap accomodation to struggling writers and artists. Renoir, Picasso and Braque were among the hopefuls who lived here. Toulouse-Lautrec's paintings provide some of the neighbourhood's most enduring images. The scenery of Montmartre was brilliantly conveyed by Maurice Utrillo, who occupied a studio in 12 rue Cortot, a 17th-century building that is now the Musée de Montmartre. Through artworks, photographs and memorabilia, the museum displays the history of the bohemian lifestyle that was characteristic of the area at the turn of the century.

Place du Tertre, adjacent to the Sacré-Cœur, remains one of the most famous places for street-artists.

The Gobelins

The extravagant interior decoration for the Palace of **Versailles** was provided by the workshop of La Manufacture des Gobelins. The Gobelin brothers began working together in 1440 and by the beginning of the 17th century the workshop had been upgraded to a factory to produce tapestries. Rather than giving endless commissions, Louis XIV acquired the workshop in 1662 and extended its repertoire to provide the decor he needed. The king was responsible for bringing together the most skilled craftsmen, including cabinet-makers, silversmiths and carpet-weavers. Gobelins subsequently achieved universal fame. The Savonnerie was originally in business making carpets, but was incorporated into the Gobelins factory in the 19th century.

The Gobelins continues today to make private commissions using traditional methods. A guided tour is available of the factory at work.

Notes

Musée Rodin

Auguste Rodin (1840–1917) was born in Paris. His artistic career initially depended on civic and corporate commissions, although towards the late 19th century he was established as a colossus of his genre, through sculptures that have an intense vitality and sense of emotion. Rodin lived in the Hôtel Biron, a beautiful 18th-century mansion, as a 'guest' of the State, in return for agreeing to bequeath his works to the nation. The museum has some of his finest works – *The Kiss*, *The Thinker* and *The Gates of Hell*. The garden is also a poignant setting for his work.

The Pompidou Centre

The Centre National d'Art et de Culture Georges Pompidou was constructed 1972–7 and considered 'state of the art' for its time, though a popular reaction now may well be 'look at the state of it'. Designed by British architect Richard Rogers and the Italian Renzo Piano, structural elements such as lifts, escalators, and massive air ducts feature on the outside in order to maximise exhibition space on the inside.

The Centre houses the **Musée Nationale d'Art Moderne**, with its collection of modern masters such as Dali, Warhol, Kandinsky and Picasso, covering movements such as Fauvism, Cubism, Surrealism and Expressionism. The exhibition is spread over two floors of the centre, and at any one time has up to 800 items from its collection of 35,000 on display. The collection contains work dating from 1905 to the present day and is generally regarded as continuing chronologically from the work exhibited at the **Musée d'Orsay**. In such a small number of artworks it manages to convey the essence of each of the various artistic movements to have held sway this century.

Sculpture plays its role in the display, with work by Marcel Duchamp, which in its time challenged perceptions of what constitutes art. Contemporary exhibitions are held on the top floor and, like the rest of the work exhibited here, always constitutes a liberal view of art.

The most important exhibits include the work of Marquet, Matisse, Vlaminck and Chagall, Van Gogh, Picasso, Braque, Cézanne and Duchamp, to name but a few of the better known artists.

Also in the centre is a graphic, commercial and industrial design section, a public library, a workshop for children specialising in art, and an institute specialising in acoustics and music.

Outside the centre a giant digital clock counts down the seconds to the start of the next millennium and in the **Stravinksy Fountain**, the sculptural works of Niki de Saint-Phalle and Jean Tinguely are displayed.

NOTES

ART, DESIGN & MUSIC

Theatre & Music

Entertainment of any kind is never in short supply in Paris. The city boasts a number of theatres, all producing a range of styles and performances to suit almost any taste, from highbrow classical works to *avant garde* contemporary productions. Paris has a long-established reputation for playing host to touring companies from overseas who frequently perform in their native language.

It was here that the **Comédie Française**, the world's oldest national theatre company and the pillar of modern French theatre, was founded. The season runs from September through to July, when the company performs mainly classical drama interspersed with contemporary works from new playwrights.

Lovers of music are well catered for in Paris, with a good selection of styles for all audiences. The **Opéra de Paris Bastille**, opened in 1989, is the high-tech home of the **Opéra de Paris**. Its design and construction has made the Bastille the most controversial opera house in Europe, since it defies all traditional notions of lavish interiors with its functional and stark upholstery, monochromatic design scheme and curved glass building. Opera can also be heard at the **Opéra Comique**, the **Théâtre du Chatelet** and the **Théâtre des Champs-Elysées**.

Music thrives in Paris; a rush of government spending and promotion has ensured that the tradition will remain a lively one. Many churches serve as performance places for small ensembles and chamber music concerts, providing an ideal backdrop in which to listen to classical music. In addition the **Museé de Orsay** and the **Louvre** both have auditoria specifically designed for performances.

Decorative art

Paris has always been known as a source of style, not only in its fashions but in its buildings, gardens and general architecture. Many notable buildings with parts dating as far back as the 12th and 13th centuries still exist today as examples of medieval and Gothic architecture. The church of **St-Martin-des-Champs** dates from 1130 and is typical of its period, with rounded walls, open radiating chapels and decorative motifs. **Notre Dame** is the best known example of Gothic architecture, but other notable examples worth seeing include **Sainte-Chapelle**, and the **Tour de Jean-Sans-Peur**.

The **Place des Vosges**, constructed in the 17th century, is a feat of architectural unity – 36 symmetrical houses in the grandest style of the day. Squares were a feature of the period, with other notable sites including **Place Dauphine**, **Place de la Concorde** and **Place des Victoires**. Additional building and improvements to the Palace of the **Louvre** including the addition of a baroque style colonnade in the 17th century, and the construction of **Versailles** and the **Hôtel des Invalides** meant building works on a huge scale were never far from public awareness.

The architecture of the Enlightenment in the latter half of the 18th century looked back to classical traditions, but the façades, colonnades, flying buttresses, and ornate and decorative mouldings were simplified to reflect the more modern era. After the Revolution the increased size of the population dictated changes in urban planning – four-storey buildings were added to the landscape, but the obsession with classical traditions continued, particularly with the addition of the Arc de Triomphe and the façade of the Assemblée Nationale. The wide boulevards built to help control angry, rioting mobs improved hygiene and the addition of street lighting created districts that were pleasant to walk in. The regeneration of Paris under Haussmann featured more sober decoration and a scheme of building which blended with the surrounding areas – a stark contrast to the cast iron and glass structures that followed. Street-lamps, doorways, balconies and cafés are just some of the Art Nouveau heritage throughout the city, and if you are shopping look out for the wonderful stained glass dome at **Galeries Lafayette**. Guru of the genre, Hector Guimard (1867–1942) left a wonderful legacy of métro station entrances, as at **Porte Dauphine** and **Rue des Abbesses**. **Maxim**'s, at 3 Rue Royale, provides a feast of Art Nouveau interiors as well as haute cuisine.

The **Musée des Arts Décoratifs** in the **Louvre** takes style as its theme, from the Middle Ages to whatever is currently in vogue.

Le Corbusier

Le Corbusier was the 'nom d'architecture' of Charles-Edouard Jeanneret (1888–1965). The influence of Le Corbusier on modern architecture was profound. Villa La Roche, a celebration of concrete and steel with windows placed in horizontal lines, is now **Fondation Le Corbusier**, a museum in his honour.

Cinematic art

The Lumière brothers held the first world premiere, screening a film in the Salon Indien at the **Grand Café**, on Boulevard des Capucines, in 1895. Paris remained the centre of the French film industry, with masterpieces such as *Les Enfants du Paradis*, and Abel Gance's *Napoléon*. The **Musée du Cinéma**, established by the enthusiast Henri Langlois in 1936 without State funding, is a brilliant collection of memorabilia and costumes which help trace the history of cinema from the early days of magic lanterns, peep shows and silent movies to the big screen era of Hollywood.

NOTES

Denis Diderot (1713–84)

WRITERS & PHILOSOPHERS

Voltaire

'Literature is nothing without a friend, but an illiterate friend is dry company,' said Voltaire (1694–1778). Born in Paris as François-Marie Arouet, his earliest achievement was second place in the Academie Française's inspiring challenge to write a verse on restoring Notre Dame's choir. Thereafter establishing himself as one of Europe's key intellectuals, he wrote plays, histories and satires. Voltaire is regarded as one of the three greatest writers of the 18th century. By his contemporaries he was regarded as the best tragic writer of his day, ironic since nowadays he is regarded as the writer producing work most representative of his times than any other author. His ridicule of the Duc d'Orléans (then the Regent) earned him his first spell in the **Bastille** in 1717. Similar sentences followed, and libel actions even forced him into occasional exile.

> Innumerable high-dressed gentlemen are gone to inorganic powder, with no comfortable or profitable memory to be held of them; yet this poor Voltaire, without implement except a tongue and brain, is still a shining object to all the populations, and they say: 'Tell us of him, he is the man.'
>
> Thomas Carlyle (1795–1881,) essayist and historian

Molière

Molière was the stage name of Jean-Baptiste Poquelin (1622–73), who was born in Paris, and began his professional life with a law degree, but thereafter founded the Illustre Théâtre (1643) and began treading the boards around France. The company was incorporated into the National Theatre (the **Comédie Française**), established in 1680 by Louis XIV, providing a showcase for playwrights such as Racine. Molière's works spanned various genres: satire, farce, verse and prose, with *Le Misanthrope* (1666) one of his most enduring plays.

> He was delighted with Molière, who made him acquainted with the customs of Paris, and indeed of the human race.
>
> Voltaire, *L'Ingénu*, 1767

NOTES

Balzac

Honoré de Balzac (1799–1850) was born in Tours and studied law in Paris from 1816 to 1819, before becoming a writer. Despite his immense *La Comédie humaine* (The Human Comedy), a collection of more than 100 works tracing the social, political and economic developments after the 1798 Revolution, he was never accepted by the august Académie Française. He achieved notoriety in 1829 when he published the successful *La Physiologie du mariage*, a glib look at society. His own style of writing - 'de Balzac' - was established in 1830 and from then on his ambition to produce a full descriptive account of the whole of society earned him a reputation for prolific work.

Many authors use a pen name for writing, but Balzac assumed other identities as a ploy to avoid creditors. Another was the use of a secret entrance to his house on Rue Raynouard, which is now a museum, **Maison de Balzac**. A statue of Balzac by the Boulevard Montparnasse is a great tribute from sculptor Auguste Rodin.

Gaudrissart, a character from
La Comédie humaine

Flaubert

Gustave Flaubert (1821–80) was born in Rouen, arriving in Paris to study law, but was soon forced to leave his studies, and Paris, due to an inexplicable illness. He turned instead to writing, and became known as both a Realist and a Romantic, though the moral (or rather 'immoral') tone of *Madame Bovary* (1857) shocked the public. His *Sentimental Education* was an influential French novel of the 19th century.

> I have been hard at work on a novel of modern life
> set in Paris … I want to write the moral history,
> or rather the sentimental history, of men of my
> generation. But I'm also afraid that my
> background will eat up my foreground, that is the
> trouble with the historical novel. Historical figures
> are more interesting than fictional characters.
> Gustave Flaubert to a friend in 1848

Maupassant

Godson of Flaubert, Guy de Maupassant (1850–93) excelled at writing short stories, and detailing various aspects of Parisian life. In his early career he wrote poetry (*Des vers*, 1880), travel journals and short stories. He wrote six novels, of which the best known is *Pierre et Jean* (1888). Maupassant's tomb is in the **Montparnasse Cemetery**, where he lies alongside many other artists and literary figures.

Victor Hugo

The tragedy of the Parisian poor was movingly portrayed in *Les Misérables*, Victor Hugo's (1802–85) epic novel published in 1862. During the 1830s and '40s Hugo lived and wrote at 6 Place des Vosges. He began writing at the age of 13 and is widely regarded as the driving force in the Romantic movement of the 1830s and '50s. He wrote ballads, poems, odes, drama and novels, achieving fame with the stage performance of *Hernani*. Hugo's opposition to Louis Napoléon resulted in exile, though he maintained a presence in the capital with literary attacks such as *Napoléon le petit*, published in 1852. It was in Guernsey that he wrote some of his greatest poetry. *Les Chatiments* was published in 1853 and *La Fin dé Satin* in 1856. The fall of the Second Empire facilitated his return to Paris in 1870, when he was welcomed as the grandee of French literature. He died in 1885, and is enshrined in the Panthéon. The house is now a museum in his honour.

Zola

Emile Zola (1840–1902) began his working career as a journalist and dabbled in writing short stories and poetry. His work was systematically scorned by the Establishment until he adopted a new style of writing under the influence of Balzac and Taine, loosely termed Naturalism. Zola was a prolific author and an influential political and social writer. In his lifetime he wrote 31 novels, 20 of which make up the *Rougon-Macquart series*, literary criticism, plays, five collections of short stories as well as commentary on society as a political journalist. Among his most well-known works are *L'Assommoir* (1877) and his trilogy *Les Trois Villes* published 1894–98.

Proust

The dazzling Parisian *beau monde* was recreated by Marcel Proust (1871–1922) in *A la recherche du temps perdu* (*Remembrance of Things Past*). Frequently cited as the greatest literary work ever, it details a Parisian life of salons, snobbery, love, courtesans and intrigue. Living on the Boulevard Haussmann, Proust became increasingly reclusive. Suffering from asthma, he wrote through the night in a cork-lined room, and slept during the day. His bedroom has been reconstructed in the **Musée Carnavelet**.

NOTES

Foreign writers in Paris

Paris has always been a beacon for writers, who have gathered here from around the world in search of like-minded spirits, inspiration and, ultimately, publishers.

One of the most famous literary exiles was Oscar Wilde (1854–1900), who was born in Dublin and studied at Oxford University. His reputation was established with *The Happy Prince* (1888), though he is best remembered for the wit of plays such as *Lady Windermere's Fan* (1892), *The Importance of Being Earnest* (1895) and *A Woman of No Importance* (1893). After a legal dispute with the Marquis of Queensberry, over his affair with the Marquis' son, Lord Alfred Douglas, Oscar Wilde spent two years in Reading Gaol, and then moved to Paris in 1897. He is buried in Père-Lachaise Cemetery.

The 1920s saw Gertrude Stein (1874–1946) established as a key figure of the international literary set, receiving in her Parisian flat the likes of James Joyce, Scott Fitzgerald and Ernest Hemingway. Hemingway (1899–1961), one of America's most celebrated authors, drew on his Parisian memoirs to write *A Moveable Feast* (1964), while *The Sun Also Rises* (1926) gives another perspective on Americans living in Paris.

Other notable writers to have resided in Paris include Irish-born Samuel Beckett, who wrote in French then translated his text back into English. In 1969 he won the Nobel Prize for Literature.

Ezra Pound (1885–1972), born in Idaho, USA, first moved to Venice, then London, before moving on to Paris, then finally settling in Italy. He is best known for his poetry and a new movement for the era known as imagism, in which text is sparse, descriptions brief and economical but full of vitality and meaning.

Richard Wright (1907–60), a black American playwright whose works were a protest against the racism in the South, spent much of his time from 1946 in Paris. His first novel, *Uncle Tom's Children* (1938), was later succeeded by non-fiction and autobiographical writing.

GREAT PARISIAN FIGURES

St Geneviève

The patron saint of Paris, St Geneviève began life in 422 as the daughter of a wealthy Gallo-Roman landowner in Nanterre. Taking religious orders in Paris, St Geneviève was in the city when Attila's Huns approached in 451. Assuring Parisians that they would be saved from these barbarians, she spent all her waking hours praying for a successful outcome. Paris was spared: she thanked God and Paris hailed her as a miraculous prophet. No credit seems to have gone to Actius, the Roman general, who was well prepared for an onslaught that never came. Canonised after her death, St Geneviève's feast day is 3 January.

St Denis

St Denis, the first bishop of Paris, was beheaded in 287 by the Romans for desecrating several statues of their gods. According to folklore, he simply picked up his head and walked away – 6000 steps to be precise – though other repo[rts] say he walked 6 km (4 miles) to a nearby village before bein[g] buried by his followers. He is now the patron saint of Franc[e]. The **Basilica of St Denis** is just outside the centre of Pari[s]

NOTES

Sarah Bernhardt

Sarah Bernhardt is still playing *Phèdre*, one of her greatest roles, albeit through a statue in **Place Malesherbes**. Born in Paris in 1844, her acting debut was in 1862, and her career was characterised by a tempestuous character, and eccentricities such as sleeping in a satin-lined coffin. With her innovative style she inspired Oscar Wilde to compose a poem in her honour.

Phèdre – To Sarah Bernhardt

How vain and dull this common world must seem
To such a One as thou, who should'st have talked
At Florence with Mirandola, or walked through
         the cool lives of the Academe:
Thou should'st have gathered reeds from a green
              stream
For goat-foot Pan's shrill piping, and have played
         with the white girls in the
Phaeacian glade where grave Odysseus wakened
           from his dream.
Ah, surely once some urn of Attic clay held thy
           wan dust, and
Back to this common world so dull and vain,
For thou wast weary of the sunless day, the heavy
          fields of scentless asphodel,
The loveless lips with which men kiss in Hell.

Oscar Wilde (1854–1900)

Piaf

'Non, je ne regrette rien,' sang Edith Piaf (1915–63), who certainly had plenty of cause for regret. Born in the doorway of 72 rue Belleville, the daughter of a street entertainer and a circus acrobat, she began her own life as an impoverished street singer. Her big break came when she was heard by Louis Leplée, who owned the chic cabaret spot Gerny's. He also gave her the name Piaf, colloquial Parisian for 'little sparrow'. Still untrained, she conquered the world with songs capturing the tragic, lovelorn lives of poor Parisians. A visit to **Musée Edith Piaf** is accompanied by appropriate background music. Edith Piaf rests in the **Père-Lachaise Cemetery** (named after Louis XIV's confessor), on a hill above the city, alongside the likes of Frédéric Chopin and Honoré de Balzac.

NOTES

Madame de Pompadour

1745 was a great year for Jeanne-Antoinette Poisson, a Parisian bourgeoise who became better known as Madame de Pompadour (1721–64). Meeting Louis XV at a masked ball, she was astute enough to reveal her abundant beauty. And before she could say 'I'm already married', she was established at Versailles, not to mention being ennobled as a marquise. Remembered chiefly as the king's mistress, Madame de Pompadour was also highly influential in the king's choice of ministers. She was a great patron of the arts, with Voltaire among her circle. However, opinions varied. Thomas Carlyle described her as 'a highly rouged, unfortunate female, of whom it is not proper to speak without necessity'.

Cemeteries

For those with chasing the spirit of the past, Paris has three major cemeteries where the great and good are buried. Even if your interest is only fleeting, the cemeteries are a pleasant place to stroll and contemplate. **Père-Lachaise Cemetery** is a good starting point for the curious. Among the many legendary figures buried here are Abélard and Héloise, Chopin, Balzac, Bizet, Edith Piaf, Jim Morrison, Oscar Wilde and Proust, to name but a few. The cemetery has a political history too: along the Mur des Fédérés – one of the cemetery walls – almost 150 survivors of the Paris Commune of 1871 were systematically lined up and shot.

Montmartre Cemetery, true to the spirit of the area, is the final resting place of many artists including Berlioz, Degas, Zola, Nijinsky, Toulouse-Lautrec's model La Goulue and Alphonsine Plessis, who inspired Verdi's *La Traviata* and Dumas' *La Dame aux Camélias*.

The last of the three, **Montparnasse Cemetery** contains the tombs of Captain Dreyfus, Jean-Paul Sartre, Simone de Beauvoir, Maupassant and Baudelaire.

RIVER LIFE

The Seine

The river splits the city into two – the Left Bank is on the south and the Right Bank is to the north.

The Seine was originally a trade route and the main highway to Paris, with many foodstuffs and commodities being unloaded at **St-Nicolas Port** by the **Louvre**. Barges also carried human cargo and were a cheap form of transport until the advent of trains. Nowadays, goods are still brought into the city by river, and tourists enjoy the sights from *bateaux mouches*.

The river has a grimy history. The polluted waters were used as a dumping ground for the factories which once operated on the river bank. Washerwomen worked, animals and people bathed and the water was drunk in this uncleaned state by all Parisians.

Today the river has changed its character, the factories have been moved away from the river banks. Plant life and fish have been reintroduced to the river.

A river may be timeless, but its banks are a different story. Not far from the **Eiffel Tower**, the redevelopment of the **Quai de Grenelles** was vehemently criticised for its similarity to the New York skyline in miniature.

NOTES

Left and Right Banks

The Seine divides Paris into the Rive Gauche (left bank), with its intellectual and bohemian character, while the Rive Droite (right bank) is the commercial heart.

> We went today along the Boulevard Sévastopol, Rive Gauche, to pay a call. I knew the district well about six years ago, when it was a network of narrow tortuous streets; the houses high, irregular, picturesque, historical, dirty and unhealthy. The street in which our friend lived was old and narrow; the trottoir was barely wide enough for one uncrinolined person to walk on; and it was impossible to help being splashed by the passing carriages … I could not help wondering how people bore to live in the perpetual noise, and heavy closeness of atmosphere.
>
> Elizabeth Gaskell, *French Life*, 1862

Bateaux mouches

One of the best ways to see Paris is from one of the *bateaux mouches* which cruise the Seine. They come in various sizes and styles: open top to enjoy the weather, as well as enclosed so that rain need not prevent the journey. They also come in various degrees of grandeur; some will serve you dinner with background music, using their powerful floodlights to illuminate the view. Stops are by the main bridges.

> The sun was setting behind a red cloud, and, while the background was filled with a light haze, a shower of gold dust, of golden dew, fell on the right bank of the river, in the neighbourhood of the Madeleine and the Tuileries. There came a moment when a ray of sunlight, gliding from between two clouds, was so resplendent that the houses seemed to flare up and melt like an ingot of gold in a crucible.
>
> Emile Zola, *The Kill*, 1872

> Paris, Rouen and Le Havre are one city, with the Seine as their street.
>
> Napoleon Bonaparte (1769–1821)

The bridges of Paris

Historically, many Parisians lived on the bridges, which were traditionally built with houses. **Pont Neuf** was the first to be built 'sans maisons' (without houses) and is the oldest-surviving bridge in Paris. Inaugurated in 1607 by Henri IV (whose statue stands on the bridge), it links the **Ile de la Cité** with both left and right banks of the Seine. In 1985 it was 'upholstered' in fabric by wrap-artist Christo.

Named after the Russian Tsar, **Pont Alexandre III** was completed in 1900, celebrating the 1893 Franco-Russian alliance and the 1900 Universal Exhibition. The bridge links

Cours La Reine and **Quai d'Orsay**. Its wealth of Art Nouveau decoration includes cherubs and winged horses, with lamps that are replicas of those on St Petersburg's Trinity Bridge. The columns at either end of the bridge seem decorative, but play a more important and technical role in the engineering of the bridge. This was the first bridge to cross the Seine in a single span.

> Of all the bridges which ever were built, the whole world who have passed over the Pont Neuf must own, that it is the noblest—the finest—the grandest—the lightest—the longest—the broadest that ever conjoined land and land together.
>
> George Moore, *Memoirs of My Dead Life*, 1906

NOTES

Ile St-Louis

Ile St-Louis, now one of the choicest addresses in Paris, was originally marshland, with few inhabitants before the 17th century other than fishermen and washerwomen. Residential development began in the 1620s, after Louis XIII commissioned the **Pont Marie** to link the island with the mainland in 1614. Elegant hôtels (town houses) and quays made it a highly desirable area right from the start, with the architectural range now spanning Baroque, Rococo and neo-Renaissance. The island's roads are a 'grid' system, bisected by the Rue St-Louis-en-l'Ile, which is a natural terrain for promenaders with its shops, restaurants and bars.

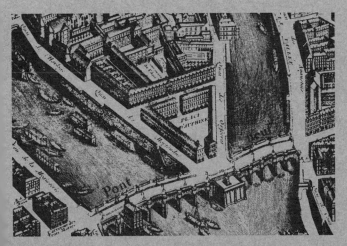

Bathing in the Seine

Bathing in floating pools moored on the Seine was a popular pastime from the 18th century, enabling Parisians to swim on the Seine without actually being in it. The last specimen was Deligny, which unfortunately subsided in 1993.

> Without stirring out of Paris it is possible to obtain the health-giving impression of sea-bathing, for all this involves is a visit to Bain Vigier, an establishment found on a pontoon moored in the middle of the Seine ... By reading the *Guide Joanne* describing the beauties of the seaside resort where you would like to be; by letting yourself be lulled by the waves created in your bath by the back-wash of the paddle steamers passing close to the pontoon; by listening to the moaning of the wind as it blows under the arches of the Pont Royal, and the dull rumble of the buses crossing the bridge just a few feet over your head; by employing these simple devices, you can produce an illusion of sea-bathing which will be undeniable, convincing and complete.
>
> Joris-Karl Huysmans, *Against Nature*, 1884

The river banks

Plenty of walkways keep you right by the river's edge. In the summer Parisians sunbathe, read newspapers and have picnics by the river, while couples kiss and cuddle all year around. If you do not want to walk, then you can see everything from a *bateau mouche*. After dark, these boats simply turn on their floodlights to illuminate the river banks, turn on the music by the dance floor, and start serving dinner.

NOTES

GREENERY

Paris in the spring-time

Paris is blessed with greenery in the form of gardens, parks, squares, or simply trees lining the boulevards. Formal, elegant parks with statues and water features, such as the **Jardin du Tuileries** and **Jardin du Luxembourg,** have been open to the public for over 300 years. The French have a love of formality in garden designs – a neat sense of order and planning, mingled with cultivated disorder in carefully arranged flower beds – man's attempts to curb nature. This type of gardening has become an artistic expression in its own right and sets the stage for the majestic buildings of the chateaux. As such the French have always regarded formal gardens as a status symbol. Parks and gardens have always had a practical function too – places to meet and socialise, to exercise and to retreat to.

The Tuileries

When Catherine de Médici, Henri II's powerful widow, purchased a disused tileworks in 1560, there was a great deal of work to be done before it became the **Jardin des Tuileries** ('tuiles' means tiles). First laid out in 1564, the gardens were not completed until 1664, when Le Nôtre succeeded his father and grandfather as head gardener at the Tuileries and gave it the streamlined look that remains. More recent enhancements include statues by Auguste Rodin. As one of Europe's first public gardens, it was a prototype for gardens throughout France.

Bois de Boulogne

The exclusive Avenue Foch leads to the entrance of the Bois de Boulogne, first used by the court for hunting before becoming a royal park at the end of the 16th century, when Louis XIV opened it to the public. Altered as part of Baron Haussmann's 'restyling' of Paris in the mid-19th century, the garden owes much to the influence of London's Hyde Park. The gardens have a less formal appearance than many French parks and are an ideal place for rowing, picnics, cycling and walking. The grounds now include a Shakespeare garden with trees and plants that appear in his plays, while for children the Jardin d'Acclimatation includes rides, a train and boat trips.

On the right (of the Bois de Boulogne), copses and low-cut plantations with reddened leaves and slender branches passed slowly by; at intervals, on the track reserved for riders, slim-waisted gentlemen galloping past, their steeds raising little clouds of fine dust behind them. On the left, at the foot of the narrow grass-plots that run down intersected by flower-beds and shrubs, the lakes, clear as crystal, without a ripple, lay as though neatly trimmed along its edges by the gardener's spades; and on the further side of this translucent mirror, the two islands, with between them the grey bar formed by the connecting bridge, displayed their smiling slopes and the theatrical outlines of fir-trees and evergreens, whose black foliage, resembling the fringe of curtains cunningly draped along the edge of the horizon, was reflected in the water.

Emile Zola, *The Kill*, 1872

Jardin du Luxembourg

Marie de Médici, who married Henri IV in 1600, nursed such nostalgia for her home town of Florence that providing her with Florentine style in Paris seemed the obvious answer. The Palais and Jardin du Luxembourg were ready for her in 1630. Unfortunately, by that time Henri IV had been assassinated and Marie banished. Nevertheless, this remains one of the city's most popular gardens. The Fontaine de Médici is 17th-century Italian style, while classical statues date mainly from the 19th century. Marie de Médici also introduced the Florentine pastime of taking horse-drawn carriage rides through parks. It was a fashion that thrived in her absence. The flower gardens are replanted three times a year and are a riot of colour, and in summer are offset with pomegranate trees, oranges, dates and rosebay.

NOTES

A Parisian garden

You fellows never knew this garden, did you? It
was like some survival from the eighteenth
century, as charming as an old lady's gentle smile.
Thick hedges separated straight narrow walks,
peaceful between two walls of carefully clipped
foliage. The gardener's shears remorselessly cut
back the branches of the dividing hedges; and here
and there one came upon flower-beds or
shrubberies as orderly as schoolboys out for a walk,
clumps of magnificent rose-bushes or symmetrical
rows of fruit trees ... I used to go there nearly
every morning and sit down and read. Sometimes
I let my book fall on my knee, to dream and listen
to the hum of Paris all around me and enjoy the
perfect restfulness of these old-world arbours.

Guy de Maupassant (1850–93), *The Minuet*

Le Parc des Buttes Chaumont

Under Napoleon III's Second Empire landscaped gardens became highly cultivated. The intention was to create 'natural' vistas within the confines of the city, for peaceful retreats and a rendezvous with nature. A triumph of imagination (and dynamite) over reality was the development of Le Parc des Buttes-Chaumont, crowned with a temple of Sybil perched on top of a 90m (300ft) cliff. The park offers panoramic views over Paris, and contains caves with stalactites, pathways leadings deep into undergrowth and the ubiquitous range of follies. **Le Parc Montsouris** follows Buttes-Chaumont's principles, and no one would ever guess that it used to be a quarry.

NOTES

Jardin des Plantes

Despite their beauty, botanical gardens were initially reserved for scholars. The Jardin des Plantes was established in the 1630s as a herb garden by Louis XIII's physicians, and became a public garden ten years later. Among endless varieties of flowers and plants stands one of the city's most senior trees, a cedar of Lebanon planted in 1734. The maze in the garden features a summer house, while the menagerie is set within a formal garden. The gardens have an extensive collection of geraniums, dahlias, cannas and iris. In 1793 the gardens became the **National Museum of Natural History**. Other botanical gardens to visit are **Le Jardin des Serres D'Auteuil** and **Le Parc Floral de Vincennes**.

Le Parc Monceau

For follies and grottoes you cannot beat the Parc Monceau. Inspired by English and Oriental taste, it was created by Louis XVI's brother, the Duke of Chartres. An Egyptian pyramid and naumachia (a lake encircled by a splendid colonnade) are both original features, though many other original delights have vanished.

> She made Maxime stroll with her at night in the Parc Monceau in the moonlight. They went into the grotto, and sat down on the grass in front of the colonnade. But when she evinced a desire to row across the little lake, they found that the boat they saw from the house was without oars. These were evidently removed at night. This was a disappointment. Moreover, the great shadows of the gardens disquieted the lovers. They would have liked a Venetian fête to be given there, with red lanterns and a band.
>
> Emile Zola, *The Kill*, 1872

NOTES

CHATEAUX

Versailles – the palace

In contrast to its current splendour, Versailles was originally a hunting lodge built by Louis XIII, which he later metamorphosed into a chateau by Philibert Le Roy. However, the intentions of Louis XIV (the Sun King) were much grander. Rather than a mere chateau, he wanted to create the ultimate palace that was a place for festivals, a shrine to his position and an example to all of Europe.

Le Vau's designs were realised between 1664 and 1670, though it was not until 1682 that Louis took up residence full time at Versailles with the entire court in tow. At any point the palace could be host to 20,000 people. Subsequent kings added their own touches, with Louis XV (who was born on the premises) upgrading the royal apartments in 1738, approached by a magnificent staircase featuring Charles le Brun's paintings.

Versailles contained everything a king could need, such as a Baroque chapel dedicated to St Louis, a 73 m (240 ft) long Hall of Mirrors, and an exquisite choice of rooms named after Roman gods. The highly marbled Apollo Room (the throne room) has an ornate ceiling, appropriately painted with a scene of Apollo in his chariot. The King's Bedchamber, where Louis XIV died in 1715, contains a painting by van Dyck, while the auditorium of the Royal Opera is a lavish affair decorated with cupids, gods, goddesses and gilt.

The last occupants of the palace were Louis XVI and Marie-Antoinette in 1789. In 1833 the chateau was opened to the public as a museum, and in 1919 it was here that the Treaty of Versailles was signed, bringing an end to World War I.

Versailles – the gardens

Lansdcape gardening reached an apotheosis in the 17th century with André Le Nôtre (1630–1700). His stunning designs for Vaux-le-Vicomte, home of Louis XIV's finance minister Nicolas Fouquet, made the king so jealous that Le Nôtre was ordered to eclipse himself at Versailles.

The grounds of Versailles are just as ornate and highly cultivated as the palace. Formal gardens provide a natural habitat for classical statues, a fountain of Neptune (which contains almost 100 spouts) and a fountain of Apollo, an orangery completed in 1686, and a temple of love (1778), which shelters a statue of Cupid beneath a dome resting on Corinthian columns.

Formal gardens were intended not only as a showcase for grand houses, but also to continue the interior design through into exterior artistry. That meant retaining complete control, and geometric shapes enclosing plants were seen as the triumph of reason over nature. Gardens were, of course, status symbols, but a belief in maintaining good health through fresh air also ensured they provided sublime walks.

Versailles –the grounds

The Grand and Petit Trianons were intended to provide inner sanctums away from the palace, where the royal family could escape the court for moments of private seclusion. Trianon is the name of a hamlet acquired (and cleared) by Louis XIV to make way for these 'satellite' palaces. The **Grand Trianon** was built in 1670 and is a masterpiece of marble and ornate panelling, with gems such as the mirror salon and the malachite salon. The **Petit Trianon**, a smaller palace, was a gift from Louis XVI to Marie-Antoinette, who took only her closest circle here.

The Hameau is a specially constructed village and toy farm (for adults rather than children), which Marie-Antoinette adored. Dressed in a simple white dress and straw hat, she played the role of a milkmaid and shepherdess, with sheep that had been especially preened and coiffed for the occasion. Nevertheless, it was also a working farm, and while the Queen merely played the role of a milkmaid, there were servants to do the real work.

Versailles

Chateau de Fontainebleau

A favourite residence of various French monarchs, this Renaissance chateau, just 65 km (40 miles) from Paris, was designed by Gilles le Breton for Francis I, though many original aspects have subsequently been remodelled. Napoleon frequently stayed at Fontainebleau, and the chateau houses a museum in his honour. Successive monarchs have added to the chateau, each bringing their own character and style to the architecture. Much of the furniture was destroyed in the Revolution, although the Throne Room modelled for Louis XV still contains the original furniture. The Fontainebleau forest was once reserved for royal hunting parties. Whilst the appearance is wild, its vast 24,700 hectares (61,750 acres) have been carefully maintained and preserved for the last seven centuries. Nowadays the 300 km (190 miles) of pathways that connect the forest with the outside world, draw tourists to lakes, ruins and caves.

Chateau de Malmaison

Malmaison is a marvellous example of Empire style – hardly surprising since the chateau was home to Empress Josephine, first wife of Napoleon, from 1799 until her death in 1814. Napoleon briefly visited the chateau during his 'Hundred Days'. Napoleon III sold the chateau in 1896, after which it became a museum housing Napoleonic memorabilia. Rooms reconstructed in the First Empire style portray the lifestyle of the Emperor. Included in the exhibits are Napoleon's throne and his death mask.

Final thoughts

DIRECTORY

Sights

Arènes de Lutèce, Rue de Navarre
Arc de Triomphe, Place Charles de Gaulle
Arc de Triomphe du Carrousel, Place du Carrousel
Bibliothèque St-Geneviève, 10 Place du Panthéon
Eiffel Tower, Champ de Mars
La Madeleine, Place de la Madeleine
La Manufacture des Gobelins, 42 Avenue des Gobelins
Montmartre Cemetery, 20 Rue Rachel
Montparnasse Cemetery, 3 Boulevard Edgar Quinet
Palais de Justice, 4 Boulevard du Palais
Palais du Luxembourg, 15 Rue de Vaugirard
Palais Royal, Place du Palais Royal
Panthéon, Place du Panthéon
Père-Lachaise Cemetery, Boulevard de Ménilmontant/16 Rue
    de Repos
Roman Baths, Crypte Archéologique, Place du Parvis Notre
    Dame
La Sorbonne, 47 Rue des Ecoles

Churches

Basilica of St Denis, 2 Rue de Strasbourg
Dome des Invalides, Avenue de Tourville
Notre Dame, Place du Parvis Notre-Dame
Ste-Chapelle, 4 Boulevard du Palais
St-Germain des Prés, Place St-Germain-des-Prés
Sacré-Cœur, 35 rue de Chevalier de la Barre/Parvis du Sacré-
    Cœur

Ste-Eustache, Place du Jour
St-Etienne-du-Mont, Place Ste-Geneviève
St-Louis-en-l'Ile, 19 bis Rue St-Louis-en-l'Ile
Ste-Séverin, 1/3 Rue des Prêtres St-Séverin
St-Sulpice, Place St-Sulpice

Museums

Conciergerie, 1 Quai de l'Horloge
Fondation Le Corbusier, 8–10 Square du Docteur Blanche
Grand Palais, Avenue General Eisenhower
Jeu de Paume, Jardin des Tuileries
Maison de Balzac, 47 Rue Raynouard
Maison Victor Hugo, 6 Place des Vosges
Musée d'Art Moderne de la Ville de Paris, 11 Avenue de
   Président Wilson
Musée des Arts Décoratifs, 107 Rue de Rivoli
Musée des Arts de la Mode, 109 Rue de Rivoli
Musée Bourdelle, 18 Rue Antoine Bourdelle
Musée Carnavalet, 23 Rue de Sévigné
Musée du Cinéma, 1 Place du Trocadéro
Musée de Cluny, 6 Place Paul Painlevé
Musée Eugène Delacroix, 6 Rue de Fürstenberg
Musée Gustave Moreau, 14 Rue de la Rochefoucauld
Musée des Invalides, Hôtel des Invalides, Esplanade des
   Invalides
Musée du Louvre (Musée des Arts de la Mode, Musée des
   Arts Décoratifs), 107 Rue de Rivoli/Cour Napoleon

Musée de Montmartre, 12 Rue Cortot

Musée National d'Art Moderne, Centre Pompidou, 6 Rue
   Beaubourg

Musée National d'Histoire Naturelle, 57 Rue Cuvier

Musée de Notre Dame de Paris, 10 Rue Cloitre-Notre-Dame

Musée de l'Opéra, 8 Rue Scribe

Musée de l'Orangerie, Place de la Concorde

Musée d'Orsay, 1 Rue de Bellechasse

Musée Edith Piaf, 5 Rue Crespin du Gast

Musée Picasso, Hôtel Salé, 5 Rue de Thorigny

Musée Rodin, Hotel Biron, 77 Rue de Varenne

Musée de la Vie Romantique, 16 Rue Chaptal

Musée du Vin, 5 Square Charles Dickens, rue des Eaux

Notre Dame Crypte Archéologique, Place du Parvis Notre
   Dame

Palais de Chaillot (Musée du Cinema), 1/17 Place du
   Trocadéro

Palais Galliera (Musée de la Mode et du Costume),
   10 Avenue Pierre 1 de Serbie

Petit Palais (Musée des Beaux Arts de la Ville de Paris),
   Avenue Winston Churchill

Theatres, Concert Halls and Opera Houses

Atelier, Place Charles Dullin

Bouffes-Parisiens, 4 Rue Monsigny

Comédie de Champs-Elysées, 15 Avenue Montaigne

Comédie Française (Salle Richelieu), 2 Rue de Richelieu

Comédie Française (Théâtre du Vieux Colombier), 21 Rue
 du Vieux-Colombier)
Hébertot, 78bis Boulevard des Batignolles
Madeleine, 19 Rue de Surène
Odéon Théâtre de l'Europe, Place de l'Odéon
Opéra Comique, 5 Rue Favart
Opéra de Paris Bastille, Place de la Bastille
Palais Royal, 38 Rue Montpensier
Théâtre du Châtelet, 2 Rue Edouard-Colonne
Théâtre National de Chaillot, Place du Trocadéro
Théâtre National de la Colline, 15 Rue Malte-Brun
Théâtre de la Ville, 2 Place du Châtelet

Parks and Gardens
Bois de Boulogne, Porte Maillot/Porte Dauphine
Jardin des Plantes, Place Valhubert/57 Rue Cuvier
Jardin du Luxembourg, Rue de Vaugirard/Boulevard Sainte-
 Michel
Jardin des Tuileries, Place de la Concorde/Rue de Rivoli
Parc des Buttes-Chaumont, Rue Botzaris/Rue Manin
Parc Monceau, Boulevard des Courcelles
Parc Montsouris, Boulevard Jourdan

Markets
Marché Biologique, Boulevard Raspail
Marché aux Fleurs, Marché aux Oiseaux, Place Louis
 Lépine/Quai de la Mégisserie

Marché aux Puces de Montreuil, Porte de Montreuil
Marché aux Puces de St-Ouen, Avenue de St-Ouen
Marché aux Puces de Vanves, Avenue Georges Lafenestre
Marché St-Germain, Rue Mabillon
Marché St-Pierre, Place St-Pierre
Marché aux Timbres, Avenue Marigny/Avenue Gabriel
Rue de Lévis, Boulevard des Batignolles
Rue de Seine and Rue de Buci

Shops
Berthillon, 31 Rue St-Louis-en-l'Ile
Brentano's, 37 Avenue de l'Opéra
Chaumet, 12 Place Vendôme
Cartier, 51 Rue François 1er
Chanel, 29/31 Rue Cambon, 42 Avenue Montaigne
Christofle, 9 Rue Royale
Compagnie Française de l'Orient et de la Chine,
   170 Boulevard Haussmann
Dior, 58 Rue du Faubourg St-Honoré, 30 Avenue
   Montaigne
Fauchon, 26–30 Place de la Madeleine
FNAC, various locations
Galeries Lafayette, 40 Boulevard Haussmann
Galignani, 224 Rue de Rivoli
Gibert Joseph, various locations
Guerlain, 68 Avenue des Champs-Elysées
Hediard, 21 Place de la Madeleine

Hermès, 24 Rue Faubourg St-Honoré
Monoprix/Uniprix, various locations
Au Printemps, 64 Boulevard Haussmann
Yves Saint Laurent, 6 St-Sulpice
La Samaritaine, 19 Rue de la Monnaie
Shakespeare & Co, 37 Rue de la Bâcherie
W H Smith, 248 Rue de Rivoli
Louis Vuitton, 6 Place St-Germain-des-Prés

Architecture
Arc de Triomphe, Place Charles de Gaulle
Basilica of St Denis, 2 Rue de Strasbourg
La Défense
Les Invalides, Avenue de Tourville
Musée de Cluny, 6 Place Paul Painlevé
Notre Dame, Place du Parvis Notre-Dame
Palais du Louvre, 107 Rue de Rivoli/Cour Napoleon
The Panthéon, Place du Panthéon
Pompidou Centre, Rue Beaubourg
Pont Alexandre III
Sacré-Cœur, 35 Rue de Chevalier de la Barre/Parvis du
    Sacré-Cœur
Tour Montparnasse, 33 Avenue de Maine

Restaurants, Brasseries and Cafés
Bofinger, 5 Rue de la Bastille
Brasserie Flo, 63 Rue du Faubourg St-Denis

Brasserie Lipp, 151 Boulevard Ste-Germain
Café de Flore, 172 Boulevard Ste-Germain
Chartier, 7 Rue du Faubourg Montmartre
La Coupole, 102 Boulevard du Montparnasse
Les Deux Magots, 170 Boulevard Ste-Germain
Le Grand Véfour, 17 Rue de Beaujolais
Lucas Carton, 9 Place de la Madeleine
Maxim's, 5 Rue Royale
Le Procope, 13 Rue de L'Ancienne-Comédie
Le Train Bleu, Place Louis Armand, Gare de Paris Lyon

Museum Quilts would like to thank the following people whose assistance contributed to the preparation of this book.

Notions Antiquaria, 24 Cecil Court, Charing Cross Road, London WC2.

Tracy Brett, 174 Oldfield Grove, London SE16.

Michael Finney, Antique Books and Prints, 11 Camden Passage, Islington, London N1.

Every effort has been made to trace copyright holders and Museum Quilts apologises in advance for any unintentional omissions. We would be pleased to insert acknowledgments as appropriate in any further edition of this publication.

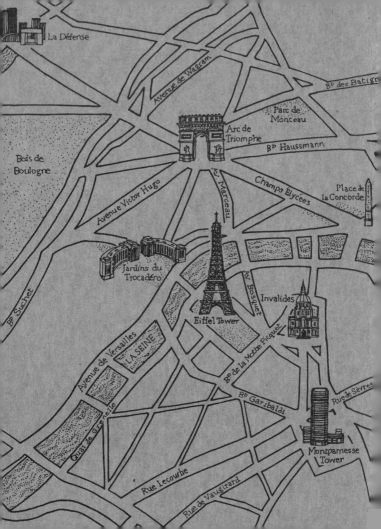